nvention

To Frances, my wife,
Without whom, nothing

domains
in language and composition

invention

John C. Adler

HARCOURT BRACE JOVANOVICH, INC.

New York   Chicago   San Francisco   Atlanta   Dallas

Jᴏʜɴ C. Aᴅʟᴇʀ was Head of the English Department at George F. Baker High School in Tuxedo, New York. He has written reviews for *The English Journal,* and is currently writing a biography of the Russian biologist Élie Metchnikoff.

Printed in the United States of America

ISBN 0–15–312300–1

ACKNOWLEDGMENTS: For permission to reprint copyrighted material, grateful acknowledgment is made to the following publishers, authors, and agents:

ATHENEUM PUBLISHERS, INC.: From *African Genesis* by Robert Ardrey, copyright © 1961 by Literat S.A. From *The Conspiracy Against Childhood* by Eda J. Le Shan, copyright © 1967 by Eda J. Le Shan. From *Confessions of an Advertising Man* by David Ogilvy, copyright © 1963 by David Ogilvy Trustee.

A.S. BARNES & COMPANY, INC.: From *A Boy and His Gun* by E.C. Janes.

GERTRUDE RYDER BENNETT: "Diary of a Raccoon" by Gertrude Ryder Bennett originally published in *The Saturday Evening Post,* April 24, 1948, copyright 1948 by The Curtis Publishing Company, from *The Harvesters* by Gertrude Ryder Bennett, published by The Golden Quill Press, Francestown, N.H., 1967.

BOOKS, INC., WASHINGTON, D.C.: From *Picture of Dorian Gray* by Oscar Wilde.

BRANDT & BRANDT: From "High Threshold" by Alan E. Nourse from *Astounding Science Fiction,* copyright 1951 by Alan Nourse.

CURTIS BROWN LTD.: From "The Tomb of Tutankhamen" from *The World of the Past,* by Howard Carter and A.C. Mace.

WILLIAM C. BROWN COMPANY, PUBLISHERS, DUBUQUE, IOWA: From *Philosophy of Recreation and Leisure,* by Jay B. Nash, copyright 1953.

THE BRUCE PUBLISHING COMPANY: From *The Gospel According to Madison Avenue* by Ray Hutchinson, copyright 1969, Bruce Publishing Company.

CAMBRIDGE UNIVERSITY PRESS: From *The Mysterious Universe* by Sir James 'Jeans.

CHANTICLEER PRESS, INC.: From *Living Insects of the World* by Alexander and Elsie Klots, published 1969 by Doubleday & Co., Inc.

THE CHRISTOPHERS: From *Government Is Your Business* by James Keller.

THOMAS Y. CROWELL COMPANY: From *Life Around Us,* by Fritz-Martin Engel, copyright © 1965 by George G. Harrap & Company, Ltd. and Thomas Y. Crowell Company, Inc.

JOAN DAVES: From *A Drum Major for Justice* by Martin Luther King, Jr., copyright © 1968 by the Martin Luther King, Jr. Estate.

THE DIAL PRESS: From *Moment in the Sun* by Robert Rienow and Leona Train Rienow, copyright © 1967 by Robert Rienow and Leona Train Rienow.

THE DIAL PRESS, INC. and GEORGE G. HARRAP & COMPANY LIMITED: From *The Fight for Food* by J. Gordon Cook, © 1957 by J. Gordon Cook.

DODD, MEAD & COMPANY, INC.: From *Adventures in Nature* by Edwin Way Teale, copyright 1945, 1959 by Edwin Way Teale. From *A Teen-Ager's First Car* by Henry Gregor Felsen, copyright © 1966 by Henry Gregor Felsen. "On the Death of Smet-Smet, the Hippopotamus-Goddess" from *The Collected Poems of Rupert Brooke,* copyright © 1915 by Dodd, Mead & Company, Inc., copyright 1943 by Edward Marsh.

DODD, MEAD & COMPANY, INC. and MC CLELLAND & STEWART LIMITED, TORONTO: "A Vagabond Song" from *Bliss Carman's Poems.*

DOUBLEDAY & COMPANY, INC.: From *Stay Alive!* by Jean Carper, copyright © 1965 by Jean Carper. From *George Washington Carver* by Rackham Holt, copyright 1943 by Doubleday & Company, Inc. From *How Does It Work?* by Richard M. Koff, copyright © 1961 by Richard M. Koff. From "The Mark of the Beast" by Rudyard Kipling, from *The Phantom Rickshaw and Other Stories* by Rudyard Kipling. From "Youth Revolt the Future Is Now," copyright © 1970 by Margaret Mead, as adapted by *The Saturday Review* taken from the chapter entitled, "The Future Prefigurative Cultures and Unknown Children" from *Culture and Commitment* by Margaret Mead.

DOUBLEDAY & COMPANY, INC. and A.P. WATT & SON, the LITERARY EXECUTOR OF W. SOMERSET MAUGHAM and WILLIAM HEINEMANN LIMITED: From *Of Human Bondage* by W. Somerset Maugham, copyright 1915 by Doubleday & Company, Inc.

DOWNE PUBLISHING, INC.: From "When Is It In and When Is It Sick?" by Judith Crist from *Ladies' Home Journal,* September 1966, © 1966 Downe Publishing, Inc.

Contents

Introduction

The skill of writing what you want to write is very valuable. But such a skill does not come easily. Its development calls for much practice.

You can't develop it by hearing a lecture or reading a book. Hearing lectures and reading books are useful, of course, but the best way to develop a skill is by doing it yourself.

It's not unlike developing the skill of riding a bicycle. You can't gain that skill by hearing a lecture or reading a book. You have to get on the bicycle and painfully pedal about.

"Getting it by doing it" is the purpose of this book. This book doesn't tell you how to do anything. It doesn't give you any rules. All it does is to present you with the opportunity to practice the skill of writing what you want to write in the way you'd like to write it.

Writing is odd. It's made up of many things. One of these things is grammar. You've studied grammar, and will continue to study it. You've studied the various details of construction, such as paragraphs, topic sentences, and organization.

What you may not have studied is creativity. But you have it just the same. How often, for instance, have you had the following experience:

You sit down, happily, or sadly, or just resignedly, to write a composition. You've been given an assignment such as: "Why I threw three coins in the fountain," or "Why having too many wavy places in a gymnasium floor is not a good thing," or "Why I believe the boy (or girl) who sits next to me will never win a beauty contest." Pretty dreary stuff, but they're assignments, and assignments can be grim things. They've got to be done. So you begin, slowly at first. Maybe you pick up momentum, maybe you don't.

But suddenly you see on the page before you, in your own handwriting, something you never intended to say. It is enormously clever. Surely you never directed your hand to write it. And yet, there it is—new, never said before, a product of your creative mind. How did it get there? Who did it? You did it.

You may argue that you've never had such an experience. Then prove to yourself that it can happen to you too. Here's a suggestion to get you started.

Begin with a word: *absent-minded*.

Add an article:	An absent-minded
Add a noun:	An absent-minded boy
Add a verb phrase:	An absent-minded boy came into the room
What did he do then?	An absent-minded boy came into the room and sat down
Where did he sit?	An absent-minded boy came into the room and sat down on a chair on which a girl was sitting.

You take it up from there.

Suppose someone shows you a photograph of an empty room and says: "Fill the room and write a page or so about what is filling it."

The technique used above, starting with the word *absent-minded* and ending with the reactions which followed when an absent-minded boy sat down on a chair occupied by a girl, could certainly fill that empty room. And you could certainly write that page or so.

Each of the 29 sections of this book is headed by a word: *Commitment, Justice, War, Hunger,* and so on. Each of these words is accompanied by a photograph which suggests that word. Several quotations follow each photograph, along with suggestions for writing. But always, if you have a better idea, by all means use it!

One more thing.

Suppose you read: "You are at a party. You are introduced to a marvelous person. In a few paragraphs, describe him."

There's something strange here. Why should this person be male? Why not female?

The explanation rests in our grammar as we use it.

Consider the last sentence of the above quotation: "In a few paragraphs, describe him." Here "him" obviously means both "him" and "her."

Now, this limitation to the pronoun "him" is due to a strange grammatical bigotry shared by many languages in addition to English: "Whenever there are both males and females present, even though they be in the proportion of 10,000,000 females to one male, the pronoun describing any one member of the group shall be masculine."

So, ladies, be generous, patient, and understanding. And always remember that because "he" or "himself" is often collective, you must go right ahead and interpret the pronoun exactly as you see fit.

—John C. Adler

2

SOCIETY

commitment

Auto Wreck

Its quick soft silver bell beating, beating,
And down the dark one ruby flare
Pulsing out red light like an artery,
The ambulance at top speed floating down
Past beacons and illuminated clocks
Wings in a heavy curve, dips down,
And brakes speed, entering the crowd.
The doors leap open, emptying light;
Stretchers are laid out, the mangled lifted
And stowed into the little hospital.
Then the bell, breaking the hush, tolls once,
And the ambulance with its terrible cargo
Rocking, slightly rocking, moves away,
As the doors, an afterthought, are closed.

We are deranged, walking among the cops
Who sweep glass and are large and composed.
One is still making notes under the light.
One with a bucket douches ponds of blood
Into the street and gutter.
One hangs lanterns on the wrecks that cling,
Empty husks of locusts, to iron poles.

Our throats were tight as tourniquets,
Our feet were bound with splints, but now,
Like convalescents intimate and gauche,
We speak through sickly smiles and warn
With the stubborn saw of common sense,
The grim joke and the banal resolution.
The traffic moves around with care,

But we remain, touching a wound
That opens to our richest horror.
Already old, the question Who shall die?
Becomes unspoken Who is innocent?
For death in war is done by hands;

Suicide has cause and stillbirth, logic;
And cancer, simple as a flower, blooms.
But this invites the occult mind,
Cancels our physics with a sneer,
And spatters all we knew of denouement
Across the expedient and wicked stones.

—KARL SHAPIRO

1. You are having breakfast. You hear the shriek of brakes, the sickening crash and crunch of metal. You rush to the window, then out to the street. There is blood and agony.

You are listening to the radio. You hear the report: "Fifteen hundred people killed in an earthquake in a Middle Eastern country."

In a few paragraphs, say whether or not there was a difference in your reaction to the two events described above.

2. You are reading the morning newspaper. You skim two items: "Five killed in two-car crash on superhighway." "Twenty cars of a passenger train derailed; list of dead growing."

You start to skim a third item. Suddenly your heart contracts, you are terrified and horrified at the same moment. You have seen a name you know: "struck by a car, is unconscious, has been taken to the hospital."

In a few paragraphs, account for the difference in your reactions to the first two news items and to the last.

COMMITMENT

You've got to be taught to hate and fear,
You've got to be taught from year to year,
It's got to be drummed in your dear little ear—
You've got to be carefully taught!

You've got to be taught to be afraid
Of people whose eyes are oddly made,
And people whose skin is a different shade—
You've got to be carefully taught.

—OSCAR HAMMERSTEIN II, from *South Pacific*

1. Strange, how some people hate mashed turnips, some people think they're okay, some people are just crazy for them.

Same way with sports, or books, or Beetle Bailey or Snoopy in the comics.

In a few paragraphs, tell: (a) of something or someone hated by somebody you know, but liked very much by you, and (b) of something or someone liked very much by somebody you know but hated by you.

2. Those somethings or someones in "a" and "b" above: trace your liking of "a" and your hating of "b" as far back into your life as you can remember. In a page or so, give the history of you and them.

3. The above passage is the lyric to a song in the musical play *South Pacific*. This lyric refers to a prejudice which someone in the play feels toward another person. "How did this prejudice arise in me?" is the question. "Was I born with it?"

The song is an answer to this question.

In a few paragraphs, tell your ideas on the same subject.

COMMITMENT

No MAN IS AN ISLAND, entire of itself; every man is a piece of the continent, a part of the main; if a clod be washed away by the sea, Europe is the less, as well as if a promontory were; . . . Any man's death diminishes me, because I am involved in mankind; and therefore never send to know for whom the bell tolls; it tolls for thee.

—JOHN DONNE, from "Meditation 17"

---

for whom the bell tolls: the church bell is rung slowly to indicate the death of a parishioner. If you hear the bell and do not know who has died, you'll send someone to find out.

---

1. This is one of the most frequently quoted passages in our language. John Donne, who wrote it in 1623, was a clergyman in London. He was very ill at the time, and thought a great deal about life and death and people.

In a page or so, tell of some of your thoughts on any one of these subjects. The topic is obviously broad, so think about a "focus" for your ideas before you write. (How did Donne "focus" his ideas?)

2. John Donne says that "no man is an island." And yet, some people certainly seem to think that they are.

In a few paragraphs, outline the story of a person who thought he was an island.

3. You are a clergyman. You feel that very few of the members of your congregation are showing the love for their fellow humans which you feel they could. So you decide to deliver a sermon next Sunday, to let them know your feelings in this regard.

Upon a page or so, write that sermon.

COMMITMENT

Where the Rainbow Ends

Where the rainbow ends
There's going to be a place, brother,
Where the world can sing all sorts of songs,
And we're going to sing together, brother,
You and I, though you're white and I'm not.
It's going to be a sad song, brother,
Because we don't know the tune,
And it's a difficult tune to learn.
But we can learn, brother, you and I.
There's no such tune as a black tune.
There's no such tune as a white tune.
There's only music, brother,
And it's music we're going to sing
Where the rainbow ends.

—RICHARD RIVE

1. This poem is by Richard Rive, who lives in South Africa. Before doing anything else, read his poem several times. Then, in a few paragraphs, say what the first four words of the poem mean to you.

2. "There's going to be a place, brother, . . ." In a paragraph or so, describe that place.

3. In a page or so, give your ideas concerning Richard Rive, author of this poem.

4. A "black tune." A "white tune." Tell about them.

5. Tell about the music which is a blend of "a black tune" and "a white tune."

COMMITMENT

THE YOUNG DO NOT KNOW what must be done, but they feel that there must be a better way.

Just how they do feel was expressed in an essay by Shannon Dickson, a fifteen-year-old Texan boy:

There is a mass confusion in the minds of my generation in trying to find a solution for ourselves and the world around us.

We see the world as a huge rumble as it swiftly goes by with wars, poverty, prejudice, and the lack of understanding among people and nations.

Then we stop and think: there must be a better way and we have to find it.

We see the huge rat race of arguing people trying to beat their fellow man out. All of this builds up, causing unrest between nations and in the home. My generation is being used almost like a machine. We are to learn set standards, strive for better education so we can follow in our elders' footsteps. But why? If we are to be a generation of repetition, the situation will be worse. But how shall we change? We need a great deal of love for everyone, we need a universal understanding among people, we need to think of ourselves and to express our feelings, but that is not all. I have yet to discover what else we need, nor have I practiced these things as fully as I should. Because when I try I'm sneered at by my elders and those who do not hear, or look at it with a closed mind. Computers take the place of minds; electronics are taking over, only confusing things more.

I admit we should follow some basic rules but first you should look at who is making the rules.

Sometimes I walk down a deserted beach listening to the waves and birds and I hear them forever calling and forever crying and sometimes we feel that way but everyone goes on with his own little routines, afraid to stop and listen for fear of cracking their nutshell.

The answer is out there somewhere. We need to search for it.

—MARGARET MEAD, from *Culture and Commitment*

Write a few pages in the manner of the above passage, telling how you see the world—its people, its problems. How are you a part of this world? What can your generation do in such a world? Before you write such an ambitious essay, notice how Shannon Dickson—who is about the same age you are—has organized his thoughts. The first paragraph of his essay outlines the problem: "mass confusion in the minds of my generation in trying to find a solution for ourselves and the world around us."

The second paragraph explains why the problem exists: "wars, poverty, prejudice, and the lack of understanding between people and nations."

The third and fourth paragraphs tell us how the problem affects the writer of this essay—and raises a series of questions which could be put into one large question: "What can I do in such a world?"

The remainder of the essay doesn't answer the question, but the writer tells us that he is going to look for an answer and for "some basic rules" to find the "better way" that Margaret Mead mentions in the introduction to the essay.

Your thoughts do not need to follow the same pattern, nor is it probable that you will see the world in exactly the same way as Shannon Dickson sees it. But your thoughts on such a weighty subject are just as important, so do your best here to present them as clearly and effectively as possible.

COMMITMENT

Is This Africa?

Is this Africa
unfair men once called
Continent of Darkness
land of baboons, apes and monkeys,
cannibals and men with tails
only fit to be
the servants of other men?

Is this the same Africa
now holding firm her own,
deciding her own fate,
with the sword of faith
fighting her foes
with weapons holier than those
used by the "master-race"?

Is this Africa
in dignity and grace
nowhere surpassed,
in wisdom deep?

Can this be the same Africa,
now center of hope,
of which men once spoke
in vilest terms?

Is this Africa,
Mother Africa,
long suppressed, divided,
ruled, impugned?
How proud are we today, Africa,
to note the part you play
for your sons and daughters
still washed in tears.

—ROLAND TOMBEKAI DEMPSTER

---

1. This poem is by Roland Tombekai Dempster, who lives in Liberia.

Someone tells you about a place, or you read about it, and you form an opinion of what it is like.

Then you see the place for yourself. It's entirely different from your previous picture of it. You find it difficult to realize that this difference exists, for you had believed what you had heard.

So, you ask a question.

In a few paragraphs, put that question into words.

2. Read the last stanza of the above poem several times, and then write a page or so saying what you feel the poet must have felt in order to have been able to write it.

13

JUSTICE

I know not whether Laws be right,
    Or whether Laws be wrong;
All that we know who lie in gaol
    Is that the wall is strong;
And that each day is like a year,
    A year whose days are long.
        —OSCAR WILDE,
            from "The Ballad of Reading Gaol"

---

gaol: jail

---

1. In the above poem we see a man's life going on, as it always does, regardless of the deeds or the reasons which brought him to the conditions in which he now finds himself.

In a page or so, give your opinions of punishment. Do you feel, for instance, that the result of punishment is improvement in the one who was punished?

2. If you've ever been shut away from life, even for a few minutes, as punishment for the doing of some deed considered wrong, tell, in a page or so, about your feelings during that shut-away period.

If you've never been so shut away, imagine that this is happening to you, and write your thoughts and feelings.

One of two brothers killed a man in
    cold blood.
But the brothers are Siamese twins.
Can the State punish the bad brother
    without doing an injustice to the
    good brother?   —"A Legal Dilemma"

1. You are the "good brother" of the above passage. In a page or so, tell what you know about the "bad brother," and what, in your opinion, led him to commit the crime of murder.

2. Surely, sometime during your life, you've been confronted by a situation in which you were (as the saying goes) "caught between the devil and the deep blue sea." You had a decision to make, and neither choice was satisfactory. In a page or so, tell about it.

3. In a few paragraphs, outline a story (different from the one in the above passage) which tells of a relationship between two people "closer than brothers or sisters."

JUSTICE

I WANT YOU TO SAY that day that I tried to be right and to walk with them. I want you to be able to say that day that I did try to feed the hungry. I want you to be able to say that day that I did try in my life to clothe the naked. I want you to say on that day that I did try in my life to visit those who were in prison. And I want you to say that I tried to love and serve humanity.

Yes, if you want to, say that I was a drum major. Say that I was a drum major for justice. Say that I was a drum major for peace. I was a drum major for righteousness.   —MARTIN LUTHER KING, JR., from Sermon delivered at Ebenezer Baptist Church in Atlanta, Georgia

1. This passage is part of a sermon given by the Reverend Martin Luther King, Jr., a man who was, surely, one of the great Americans. The sermon was one of the last that he delivered.

Martin Luther King, Jr. A great man.

In a page or so, say what, in your opinion, are the qualities of a great man.

2. The Reverend King speaks of his hope that people will think of him as having been "a drum major"—a drum major for justice, for peace, for righteousness. In other words, that he was a leader in the march toward these goals.

Henry David Thoreau, another great American, toward the end of his book *Walden*, writes: "If a man does not keep pace with his companions, perhaps it is because he hears a different drummer. Let him step to the music which he hears, however measured, or far away."

In a page or so, tell of "a different drummer" that you might have heard, and something of the nature of the "music" which came from his drum.

3. In the *New Testament* (Mark I: 3) there appear the words: "a voice of one crying in the wilderness."

In a few paragraphs or so, say what, in your opinion, is the meaning of these words.

JUSTICE

On February 18, 1965, the United States Senate Subcommittee on Administrative Practice and Procedure began hearings on the activities of government agencies that invade privacy. At the first of these hearings, one of the devices viewed with special interest was an olive with a toothpick stuck in it. This ordinarily innocent object contained a tiny transmitter; the toothpick served as its antenna. Immersed in a martini, it could broadcast the length of a city block. Thus, a receiver, located anywhere within a hundred yards or so of a cocktail party, could monitor the conversation. —SENATOR EDWARD V. LONG, from *The Intruders*

---

1. Animated cartoons, comics, movies, TV have told their tales of super sleuthing. In a page or so, invent your own sleuth.

2. One of the big problems of a democratic government like ours is this: does freedom of speech or action ever reach the point where it must be suppressed?

If we maintain these two freedoms, we maintain our democracy.

But if we never, under any circumstances, suppress them, perhaps we'll have no country.

It's puzzling.

In a page or so, discuss any personal experience you may have had with this problem. If you've never had any, construct one.

3. You have done a horrible deed, and must get away without anyone knowing when or how you left, or where you are going.

In a page or so, recount your thoughts and actions.

The LETTER IS PASSED up to the Judge, who reads it inscrutably. Then he is ready. The clerk stands up and addresses the dock in monotone, ". . . you stand convicted of fraudulent conversion, do you know of any reason why this court shall not pass sentence upon you?"

The prisoner stands wordless.

The Judge looks at the prisoner.

"Victor Albert Crawford—what do you expect me to do with you?" There is a pause. "You have made a proper mess of your life." Another pause. "I have no choice but to send you to prison again for a long time." The prisoner makes his first gesture. "Thirty months." The prisoner opens his mouth but the warder without quite laying hands on him has him away from the rail and into the back of the dock and down the trap door; he has vanished, it is over.

—SYBILLE BEDFORD, from *The Faces of Justice*

---

dock: the place in an English court where the prisoner stands or sits

fraudulent conversion: stealing

---

1. Victor Albert Crawford: a man who made "a proper mess of his life." Back he goes to prison, for two and a half years this time.

In a page or so, describe this man, and tell something of his past life.

2. The circumstances of our lives lead us here and there, very often in spite of our desires and our efforts.

In a page or so, tell of the actions of fate (for good or for bad) upon someone you have read of or known.

3. In a few paragraphs, say what, in your opinion, are the three or four most important influences upon a person's development.

WAR

On the Idle Hill of Summer

On the idle hill of summer,
  Sleepy with the flow of streams,
Far I hear the steady drummer
  Drumming like a noise in dreams.

Far and near and low and louder
  On the roads of earth go by,
Dear to friends and food for powder,
  Soldiers marching, all to die.

East and west on fields forgotten
  Bleach the bones of comrades slain,
Lovely lads and dead and rotten;
  None that go return again.

Far the calling bugles hollo,
  High the screaming fife replies,
Gay the files of scarlet follow:
  Woman bore me, I will rise.

—A. E. HOUSMAN

1. In a page or so, say what ideas ran through your mind as you read this poem.

2. Consider the first two lines of the poem: It is such a dreamy summer day. How can it possibly be that somewhere men are shrieking and killing one another?

What a terrible contrast! For one person, joy and beauty. For another, terror and death.

Tell whether or not you feel the opening lines of the poem—and the contrast they provide—make war seem all the more terrible. Tell why you feel as you do.

3. We all are well aware of war and the call that war will perhaps make upon us.

In a page or so, say what you think concerning war, or if not you yourself, what someone of your acquaintance thinks.

4. The last line of the above poem: "Woman bore me, I will rise," is based on the sentence in Job, XIV: 1, of the Bible: "Man that is born of a woman is of few days, and full of trouble."

In a brief essay, say whether or not you think man's life must be "full of trouble."

WAR

THEN A TREMENDOUS FLASH OF LIGHT cut across the sky. Mr. Tanimoto has a distinct recollection that it travelled from east to west, from the city toward the hills. It seemed a sheet of sun. Both he and Mr. Matsuo reacted in terror—and both had time to react (for they were 3,500 yards, or two miles, from the center of the explosion). Mr. Matsuo dashed up the front steps into the house and dived among the bedrolls and buried himself there. Mr. Tanimoto took four or five steps and threw himself between two big rocks in the garden. He bellied up very hard against one of them. As his face was against the stone, he did not see what happened. He felt a sudden pressure, and then splinters and pieces of board and fragments of tile fell on him. He heard no roar. (Almost no one in Hiroshima recalls hearing any noise of the bomb.)   —JOHN HERSEY, from *Hiroshima*

---

1. One of the most debated questions of the past quarter century has been: Should the United States have dropped atomic bombs upon Japan shortly before the end of World War II?

You are Harry Truman, President of the United States in July, 1945. You are in the process of making up your mind. You and you alone must make the decision. You reach a conclusion, and then issue the orders to drop the bombs.

In a page or so, tell some of the "conversation" you had with yourself.

2. In a few paragraphs, say whether and why, in your opinion, some countries should be allowed to have atomic bombs, but others should not.

24

3. Russia has the bomb. The U.S. has the bomb. England has the bomb. France has the bomb. China has the bomb. Perhaps more countries have it.

In your opinion, why, since August 9, 1945, has no country dropped an atomic bomb upon any other country?

━━━━━━━━━━━━━━━━━━━━━ WAR ━━━━━━━━━━━━━━━━━━━━━

Indictment

Come let us mock the blackman
killing the yellowman and dying
for the whiteman—but not for himself.

Mock   Mock   Mock

Praise the brave warrior with gold
and silver and bronze ornating his chest—
snuffed out the ephemeral life of the sibling
in swaddling clothing held like some treasure
in the mother's tearstained arms.

Mock   Mock   Mock

—ALVIN A. SAXON, JR.

1. One of the most valuable things we learn is that there are a great many ways of looking at the same thing, and that there are a great many people in the world looking at the same thing in different ways.
The above poem is an example of this very thing.
Reread the poem very carefully, and then begin to be four different people (one at a time, of course). Write a few paragraphs telling how you feel as each person:
(a) the blackman, killing the yellowman, and dying for the whiteman, but not for yourself
(b) the brave warrior with gold and silver and bronze ornamenting his chest

(c) the mother (with tearstained arms) holding the little child whose life has just been snuffed out (Note: "ephemeral" means "short-lived"; "swaddling cloth" is used to wrap newborn children.)

(d) yourself, having just read and written about the people in the above poem.

WAR

MONKEY BUSINESS IS DELAYING work on telephone lines being strung by Italian soldiers into occupied territory in Ethiopia.

In one instance a battle occurred between signal corps men and a gang of monkeys. Scores of the soldiers suffered bumps on the head.

When the simians appeared the soldiers greeted them with stones. That was a tactical error. The monkeys got the idea and threw the stones back.

The soldiers report that detachments of monkeys are engaged in sabotage. The animals climb the poles and try to detach the wires after they are strung.   —from *The New York Times*, 1935

---

1. People who plan wars never seem to think of everything. Unexpected problems are always coming up and have to be handled on the spot.

How about classroom tests? You think of all the questions that might be asked, and study for them. (Of course, the teacher is thinking of all the questions that you think might be asked, so that he can ask a question you didn't think would be asked!)

In a few paragraphs, tell of a classroom test on which the teacher asked a question you didn't expect.

2. Observe the third paragraph in the above passage. The soldiers made a tactical error. In a page or so, tell about some problem you were trying to solve, the solution of which was impeded by a tactical error.

3. Reread the last paragraph of the above passage. Can you find the pun within it? In a sentence or so, explain the pun. In another few sentences, make a few puns of your own.

Mᴵʟᴵᴛᴀʀʏ ɪɴᴛᴇʀᴇꜱᴛ ɪɴ ᴛᴇʟᴇᴘᴀᴛʜʏ is understandable. A spy would be able to send valuable information with no danger of detection either of the message or himself. Thought control would be a powerful offensive weapon, too, a far simpler method of forcing an enemy to surrender than bombing or other physical attack. Powerful transmitters, tuned to the frequency of human brains, would broadcast telepathic orders to surrender, and the receivers of this message would helplessly comply.

—ᴅ. ꜱ. ʜᴀʟᴀᴄʏ, ᴊʀ., from *Beyond Tomorrow*

1. You are a spy with perfect ability to transmit your thoughts to anyone. But how about language difficulties? In a few paragraphs say how you would go about sending your thoughts to a person whose language you didn't know.

2. With this telepathic ability of yours say, in a page or so, how you would spend your spare time.

3. You (the telepathic spy), meet a person who, you are certain, is a spy from the other side. Very quickly you realize that this person is as good at telepathy as you are, and that he is trying to deceive you, just as you are trying to deceive him. Write the short "conversation" which you have with him.

4. Several years before you became a telepathic spy, you were a student at Rap High School. While you were there you built up a reputation that is still famous at R.H.S. In a page or so, say what you did to gain that reputation.

27

hunger

CURRENTLY, THERE IS CONSIDERABLE EXCITEMENT among food technologists and chemists over the possibility of growing microorganisms, such as bacteria and yeast, on the black liquor derived from paper pulp manufacture, from cane and beet sugar molasses, and from crude oil and coal as a method of vitamin and protein synthesis.

—WILLIAM and PAUL PADDOCK, from *Famine 1975*

1. In other words, they're going to let the germs manufacture our food out of coal and oil and old paper products. It's pretty exciting.

Now maybe the young lambs can jump around and have fun in the farmyards, instead of ending up on the dinner table.

In a page or so, reproduce the gossip in the farmyard when this news leaks out.

2. There's always been a lot of talk about "the good old days," those times when things were much better than in these times. Even in the *Iliad*, which was written about 2,800 years ago, there is talk of "the good old days."

In a page or so, tell a story about your own "good old days."

3. The problem of enough food to feed the enormously and rapidly increasing population of the earth gets more and more horrendous.

In a few paragraphs, outline your solution to this problem.

BETWEEN THE LARGER ANIMALS like the rats and rabbits on the one hand and the insects on the other, there are many creatures which do great damage to our food supplies. The potato eelworm, for example, is already doing £2 million worth of damage in Britain every year, and it is spreading. As yet there is little we can do to stop it.

In almost every country snails and their relatives are slithering and sliding over the ground in search of succulent plant food. The damage they do is prodigious, and in some parts of the world the snail has become a pest as serious as the locust is in Africa. In tropical countries one of the worst offenders is the Giant African Snail.

As in the case of other pests, attempts are being made to find predators that can control the giant snails. Among the most promising enemies investigated is another smaller snail which destroys *Achatina* by crawling inside its shell and eating it alive. But there are dangers in setting one snail to catch another. And experiments are being carried out on isolated islands to find out what happens in a battle between the rival snails before control measures are adopted.

—J. GORDON COOK, from *The Fight for Food*

1. When you really get down to thinking about things with complete impartiality, does any one creature have more rights on this planet than any other creature? Isn't the attempt to deny food to snails a case of "might makes right," which, we are taught, is a wrong attitude?

But right or wrong, the trend seems to be in that direction.

Devote a few paragraphs to setting forth your ideas on the idea that "might makes right."

2. How about this snail? Doesn't it practice cannibalism, as described in the third paragraph of the above passage? and what about the statement that "there are dangers in setting one snail to catch another"? In a few paragraphs, speculate as to what some of those dangers might be.

3. Each night before you go to bed, you check your refrigerator. Each morning you check the refrigerator again.

You begin to notice, each morning, that there is less food in the refrigerator than there was when you checked it the previous night.

In a page or so, tell about your actions to investigate this food shortage.

HUNGER

Much of the very rapid rate of growth in world population can be attributed to man's recently acquired ability to lower death rates drastically. Such killers as plague, cholera, smallpox, and diphtheria are on the wane. In addition, such debilitating diseases as malaria have been eliminated or reduced to negligible proportions over vast areas of the world. We can be proud of these accomplishments. But, ironically, in eliminating one type of human suffering we have increased the chances for another—hunger and starvation.

—ORVILLE L. FREEMAN, from *World Without Hunger*

1. There is a condition in mathematics called "inverse proportion." Like two people on opposite ends of a seesaw: as one goes up, the other goes down. Or, the more coins you remove from your bank, the fewer remain. Or, the more questions you answer on a test, the fewer remain unanswered.

According to Orville Freeman, author of the above passage, the more people we save from death by disease, the more there are to be hungry and starve to death.

Could it be that Freeman is saying: "If the germs don't get you, starvation will"?

In a few paragraphs, give your ideas on the matter.

2. Let's go back to this "inverse proportion" mentioned above. Surely you must have lived through an example of inverse proportion during your lifetime, or known about one in someone else's lifetime— a situation in which the increase in one condition brought on a decrease in another. In a page or so, tell about it.

3. There's a sentence in the above passage: "We can be proud of these accomplishments."

In a few paragraphs, tell of a recent accomplishment of which you are proud.

HUNGER

It is almost impossible for an American to visualize the diet on which most of the world exists. Imagine, if you can, a medium-size portion of rice or cereal with a few local vegetables and possibly some fish—eaten only twice a day. On most days that's all there is. Occasionally there may be tea and perhaps a little sugar and once in a while a small amount of chicken or meat (though in a country like India the average consumption of meat is an almost nonexistent two pounds per person per year). Three quarters of all the people on earth today have never in their whole lives eaten what Americans call a square meal—that is, meat, potatoes, vegetables, bread and butter, dessert, and a beverage.

—RICHARD L. TOBIN, from "Our Half-Starving World"

1. We Americans, at least so we are told, are the blessed of the earth. There's no doubt about it. Physically, we are by far the best off—in food, drink, automobiles, housing, clothing, refrigerators, shower baths, and so on.

Does it therefore follow that we are the happiest people on earth?

In a few paragraphs, say what, in your opinion, are the basic ingredients of happiness.

2. Tell the story of an enormous feast you once attended. Use a page or so in telling of it, describing the host or hostess, the reason for giving the feast, the food you ate, and the condition in which you left the feast.

3. You have been corresponding for more than a year with a pen-pal, about your age, who lives in a land in the Far East. You receive a letter that this person is being sent to the United States for three months. You invite him to visit you for one week.

In a page or so, tell about the plans you make for that week.

■■■■■■■■■■■■■■■■ HUNGER ■■■■■■■■■■■■■■■■

14

Don't let that horse
                    eat that violin

    cried Chagall's mother

                        But he
            kept right on
                        painting

And became famous

And kept on painting
                    The Horse With Violin In Mouth

                        —LAWRENCE FERLINGHETTI

Chagall: a contemporary painter

---

1. There's something called symbolism often used by artists and writers to make an idea extremely vivid. If you see a picture in which the flag is waving over a group of people, a certain idea is immediately conveyed to you. If you read, at the end of a story, that a rainbow appeared in the sky, a certain idea is immediately conveyed to you.

In a few paragraphs, tell of the certain idea which comes to you when you see, in your mind's eye, a horse eating a violin.

2. There are many kinds of hunger.

You are a prisoner, in jail. There are many things you've lost, which you're not going to get back until you regain your freedom. At this moment you are lying on your uncomfortable bed, thinking about those things you've lost.

In a page or so, how does your thinking go?

3. As we grow older, certain of our needs change. In a page or so, tell some of the needs you had as a child, but now no longer have.

GOVERNMENT

"Hush!" said bernard suddenly, and lifted a warning finger; they listened. "I believe there's somebody at the door," he whispered.

Helmholtz got up, tiptoed across the room, and with a sharp quick movement flung the door wide open. There was, of course, nobody there.

"I'm sorry," said Bernard, feeling and looking uncomfortably foolish. "I suppose I've got things on my nerves a bit. When people are suspicious with you, you start being suspicious with them."

—aldous huxley, from *Brave New World*

1. Imagine living under constant fear that someone might be listening in on your most secret conversations!

Surely you have seen a movie, or a television program in which people knew such fear. In a page or so, relate its main events.

2. You are a member of the secret police, under instructions to snoop. In a page or so, recount your activities during one busy day or night.

3. Observe the last sentence of the above passage. In a few paragraphs, give an example of this from your own experiences or from those of an acquaintance.

Consider, for a moment, the confusion produced by this welter of government. The city of La Mirada, which straddles the Los Angeles and Orange County lines, provided a poignant example not long ago. Residents of the city with "LAwrence" telephone exchanges generally were getting their fire service from the Los Angeles County Fire Department, but they weren't all doing so. New and nervous telephone operators occasionally became confused between which did and which did not. One day, a fire was reported in the two-year-old home of the John Broadbents. The operator mistakenly put the call through to the Orange County Fire Department. The department decided the call was outside its jurisdiction and passed it along to the police department of nearby Buena Park for action.

The Buena Park Police desk made some quick checks and turned the call back to the Orange County Fire Department. Eventually, the call got to where it was supposed to go in the first place: the Los Angeles Fire Department. The LAFD had a station only two blocks from the Broadbent residence, but the house was wholly engulfed in flames by the time its engines arrived. A Los Angeles fire official testified later that the home could have been saved if the engines were dispatched correctly the moment the call was turned in.   —MITCHELL GORDON, from *Sick Cities*

---

1. "Something is terribly wrong. I don't know just what it is. In fact, I don't know anything about what it is."
"Well, why don't you ask?"
"I have asked. I have pleaded."
"Well, I'll see what I can find out."
In a page or so, tell what you found out, and how you found out.

2. You are the manager of a team, or of a group of some sort. It has done well for most of the season, but suddenly it begins to go sour.
In a page or so, say what is the source of the sourness, and the steps you take to bring back the sweetness.

3. There are some things in our lives that we can do something about. And there are some things we can do nothing about. In several paragraphs, describe a few of each.

GOVERNMENT

OUR CHIEF FAULT as individual citizens is that many of us have put aside our duty. "Let George do it" seems to be the general attitude. It has become habitual and perhaps fashionable to disdain government as something beneath us. Today the chief obstacle to good government is the widespread belief that it is a job for someone else, not for us. Many of us have dropped into the dangerous belief that others should make the sacrifices for good government while we do nothing more than sit on the sidelines and complain about how the doers are doing.

Jack Johnson, the great Negro heavyweight boxing champion, nailed the flaw in this attitude during his championship fight with Jess Willard way back in 1915. As the bout was fought under Havana's blazing summer sun, a spectator at the ringside kept up a running fire of abuse at Johnson. He criticized Johnson's style, his ancestry, his color, and finally his courage in the ring. Between rounds Johnson leaned over the ropes, smiled, and said: "Man, you're down there talking. I'm up here fighting."

—JAMES KELLER, from *Government Is Your Business*

---

1. There's a big question in the above passage, one that is at the core of our system of democratic government. (Remember, "democracy" means "government by the people.") The question: Is a citizen's job done when he votes for his representative, or should he be in there at all times, seeing that his representative is doing the things he was elected to do?

For instance: you voted for Jim Jones to be president of the sophomore class, because Jim Jones said that if he was elected he'd do, or try to do, certain things.

In a page or so, say what, in your opinion, is your duty as a good member of the sophomore class, to help bring about the changes.

2. In a page or so, tell about a person you know who is willing to "let George do it."

GOVERNMENT

BULLS ARE CONSIDERED the property of the god Epaphus—or Apis—and are therefore tested in the following way: a priest appointed for the purpose examines the animal, and if he finds even a single black hair upon him, pronounces him unclean; he goes over him with the greatest care, first making him stand up, then lie on his back, after which he pulls out his tongue to see if that, too, is "clean" according to the recognized marks—what those are I will explain later. He also inspects the tail to make sure the hair on it grows properly; then, if the animal passes all these tests successfully, the priest marks him by twisting round his horns a band of papyrus which he seals with wax and stamps with his signet ring. The bull is finally taken away, and the penalty is death for anybody who sacrifices an animal which has not been marked in this manner.

—HERODOTUS, from "The Egyptian World"

1. Specific ways of doing things have been established. Just how these specific ways were established is a matter of history, sociology, and, perhaps, many other influences. Of course, the "way of doing things" sometimes changes. When and if that change should occur, everyone has to learn all over again.

In a few paragraphs, tell your attitude toward some of the "do's and don'ts" of the world you live in.

2. You are an angry parent, standing tense at the top of the stairs. You hear your child come into the house. You storm down the stairs. While you are storming down the stairs, your child waits, and watches you. When you reach the bottom, your child says, "Parent! Go up those stairs and come down properly!"

In a page or so, recount the conversation that ensues.

3. You belong to a club that meets once each week. At one meeting each month, new names are proposed, and the owners of the names are discussed in order to determine whether or not they should be elected to membership in the club.

A.S.L. is proposed for membership. You intensely wave your arm to be recognized. You are recognized. You vigorously contend that A.S.L. should not be elected to membership.

In a page or so, recount your denunciatory speech.

■ GOVERNMENT ■

How
EVER GLOOMY THE PROSPECT, it was not in the nature of the American people to give up hope. They had come a long way in the twelve generations that had elapsed since the founding of Virginia and New England. They had seen their own house divided by the slavery struggle and the Civil War, but the house had stood. They were profoundly disturbed by the problems of world leadership to which they had fallen heir, but they were in no mood to give up. They were convinced that sometime, somehow the greater world house of which their nation had become a part would stand, and would stand as a fit abode for free men.

—JOHN D. HICKS, from *The American Nation*

---

1. For a long time you have been very interested in a certain young person. However, there are some things about this young person which deeply distress you. Those distressing things are as follows: no pride in self, no hope for the future, no trust in people.

You do your best to set this person straight.

In a page or so, tell about the distressing things and the setting straight.

2. In a page or so, write about your hopes for your country.

3. In a few paragraphs, write about your hopes for the town in which you live.

Freedom

THERE WAS ONCE an old soldier who, after serving the Tsar faithfully for many long years, was finally released and sent on his way without so much as the price of a sucked egg. And as he journeyed disconsolately homeward, his legs felt tired and his feet grew sore and he stopped and sank down wearily beside a lake.

"Well," he reflected gloomily, "what am I to do now? I have no money, no food, no roof over my head, and am still many miles from home. At such a time a man feels like hiring himself out to the Devil!"

No sooner had he uttered these words, than a tiny, hairy, and incredibly ugly devil popped out of the lake and sprang ashore.

"Greetings, Soldier!" said the newcomer.

"What do *you* want?" asked the Soldier.

"Did you not say you were thinking of hiring yourself to the Devil? We'll pay you well if you do, you know!"

The Soldier scratched the back of his head and thought the matter over.

"What sort of things would I have to do for you?" he asked cautiously.

"*Do?* You won't have to *do* anything—quite the contrary in fact. All that is required is that you undertake not to wash, shave, comb your hair, cut your nails, wipe your nose, or change your clothes for the space of fifteen years. And in exchange for this we will provide you with anything you ask of us for the same term."

—from "The Soldier Who Did Not Wash," a Russian folktale

1. How about that!

You are back at the time (if you've ever left it) when not bothering to keep neat and clean seemed the most wonderful thing in the world.

In a page or so, tell your thoughts while you were being instructed to "get to that sink, quick!" Also your thoughts while getting there, being there, and leaving there.

2. In a few paragraphs, say what would be your choice if you could have only one wish.

3. In a few paragraphs, give your opinion of people who do little washing and less work.

THE LIFE OF MAN, viewed outwardly, is but a small thing in comparison with the forces of Nature. The slave is doomed to worship Time and Fate and Death, because they are greater than anything he finds in himself, and because all his thoughts are of things which they devour. But, great as they are, to think of them greatly, to feel their passionless splendor, is greater still. And such thought makes us free men; we no longer bow before the inevitable in Oriental subjection, but we absorb it, and make it a part of ourselves. To abandon the struggle for private happiness, to expel all eagerness of temporary desire, to burn with passion for eternal things—this is emancipation, and this is the free man's worship.

—BERTRAND RUSSELL, from "A Free Man's Worship"

---

1. The first sentence of the above passage is interesting. Bertrand Russell says, "The life of Man, viewed outwardly, is but a small thing in comparison with the forces of Nature."

If a man's life can be viewed outwardly, it must be possible to view it inwardly. And since Russell says that when a man's life is viewed outwardly it is a small thing in comparison with the forces of Nature, then it would seem that viewed inwardly, a man's life is not a small thing.

Here's a strange thought. When you think of something outwardly, it's one thing. When you think of it inwardly, it's another.

For instance: a mother says to her child, "Don't climb that tree, it's very dangerous." That's the outward statement. The child says to itself, "No tree is dangerous to a climber as skillful as I am." That's the inward statement.

We've started a small story. In about two pages, finish the story.

2. There are a great many more ideas in the above passage. Pick out one of these ideas that appeals particularly to you, and write a few paragraphs for or against it. For instance, do you believe that when a man bows to the inevitable he becomes a slave? What are some of the things that are devoured by Time and Fate and Death? What are some of the things that cannot be devoured by Time and Fate and Death?

If it should happen that none of the ideas in the passage appeals to you, write upon some philosophical idea which you have often wondered about.

THE ZOOLOGISTS HAD TAKEN thirty male mice and caged them in groups of three each. Within each group of three, dominance was determined by such means as tail-biting and direct attack, and subordinance by squealing and submissive postures. Within three days the dominant male was recognizable in each of the ten cages, not only on the part of the zoologists but on the part of the dominated mice. —ROBERT ARDREY, from *African Genesis*

1. Assuming that the experiment described in the above passage is representative of the world of humans as well as the world of mice, discuss, in a page or so, the following question: "Who is really free?"

2. The word "charisma" is much used these days to describe a person who has, in large quantity, the power to fascinate and to lead others.
    In a page or so, describe the person you have encountered during your lifetime who has the most charisma.

3. In a few paragraphs, say why you would rather be a leader than a follower (or *vice versa*).

Refugee in America

There are words like freedom,
Sweet and wonderful to say.
On my heartstrings freedom sings
All day every day.

There are words like brotherhood
That almost make me cry.
If you had known what I've known,
You'd know why.
                    —LANGSTON HUGHES

1. Langston Hughes, author of the above poem, was born in 1902. He died in 1967. That he is a lover of freedom is evident from the first stanza of the poem.

The second stanza may seem a little puzzling. But not when you know that Hughes was black.

In a few paragraphs, give your thoughts on the second stanza of this poem.

2. The word "freedom" of which Hughes speaks: what is there about it that makes those seven letters throb with emotion? In a page or so, tell of some creature that really appreciated freedom.

3. There is a long poem by Lord Byron entitled "The Prisoner of Chillon," which tells of the imprisonment of a Swiss political leader. The first two lines read:

"Eternal Spirit of the chainless Mind!
Brightest in dungeons . . ."

In a paragraph or so, tell what is, in your opinion, the meaning of these lines.

FREEDOM

"I KNOW HOW YOU FEEL, dear, and I'm glad you're showing me. But you'll have to show me in some other way. I can't let you pull Meatball's tail."

"I can't let you slap baby brother!"

"I can't let you shoot BB shots at the kittens."

"You may not pull the curtains down, or throw ash trays at the chandelier."

"You may not put crayon marks all over the wallpaper." . . . "You may not hit daddy with that hairbrush!"

—DOROTHY WALTER BARUCH, from *New Ways in Discipline*

---

1. You have a choice here: either you are the parent who is speaking in the above passage, or you are the child.

Whichever you are, write a page or so recounting *not* what you said aloud, but what ran through your mind while you were saying it.

2. Here's the "generation gap" again! In your opinion, is there really an unbridgeable gulf of understanding between children and their parents? If you feel that there is a real gap, give your ideas as to how that gap can be bridged. If you feel that the gap is only imaginary, give your ideas as to how to clear up this mistaken idea. A few paragraphs will do.

3. What a problem it is for an honest, loving guardian of the welfare of a young creature (for instance, a child, a puppy, or otherwise)! You want to help it to develop habits of acting and thinking which, on the one hand, will bring happiness and freedom, but which, on the other hand, will not lead to its hurt, or the hurt of other people.

In a page or so, construct a situation in which you are the guardian of the welfare of a young creature. What rules of behavior will meet the needs described above?

FREEDOM

A Vagabond Song

There is something in the autumn that is native to my blood—
Touch of manner, hint of mood;
And my heart is like a rhyme,
With the yellow and the purple and the crimson keeping time.

The scarlet of the maples can shake me like a cry
Of bugles going by.
And my lonely spirit thrills
To see the frosty asters like a smoke upon the hills.

There is something in October sets the gipsy blood astir;
We must rise and follow her,
When from every hill of flame
She calls and calls each vagabond by name.

—BLISS CARMAN

1. The English word "vagabond" comes from the Latin word *vagari*, meaning to stroll about, to wander. Surely you know the desire. Without doubt, it hits you in the spring as well as in the autumn.

It is a day in early May. A fly buzzes close to the ceiling. The sun-gorged young green leaves dance upon the tree just outside the window. The teacher tells you that run-on sentences are acts of wickedness which will not be tolerated.

You become a vagabond—at least, your mind does. In a page or so, describe your thoughts.

2. In the first line of the above poem, Bliss Carman says that something about the autumn is native to his blood, and spends the rest of the poem trying to say what that "something" is.

Is there something (other than a season of the year) that is native to your blood? If so, cover a page or so with a description of what it is. If not, tell about something that is native to the blood of one of the members of your family.

3. In a few paragraphs, tell which season of the year brings the things that you like best.

ECOLOGY

nature

ALL NATURE IS A WEB, each animal and plant a separate point where the strands come together. Pull at any individual, and the whole web is affected. Physicists tell us that every time a man or a grasshopper leaps into the air, the entire earth moves in the opposite direction. Our physical world shifts an immeasurably short distance as its reaction to either a single man or a grasshopper; but it moves. And the biological world reacts to the disappearance of a single bumblebee—even if the change is immeasurably small. —LORUS and MARGERY MILNE, from *The Balance of Nature*

1. The word is "interdependence," but not only in nature—in school, for instance, in a baseball or a basketball team, in a squad of cheerleaders, on a picnic.

In a page or so, describe an instance of interdependence in which you have played a part.

2. There are some people who seem to be so high up, so far removed in their importance, that it seems impossible that any action of yours could possibly affect them.

But the "impossible" has happened. An action of yours has affected the great, important person.

In a page or so, tell why and how the person was great and important, and what the action which affected him was.

3. In a few paragraphs, tell about an animal that has played a vitally important part in the life of someone you know.

Diary of a Raccoon

Here on this open, ancient book
Of sand beside a fern-bound brook,
Inscribed by paws all silver tipped
Upon a moonlit manuscript

In writing cuneiform and bold
The raccoon's diary is told.
Here in a silent pool of night
The polliwogs were stirred to fright—
A score of comets, fat and black,
Scurried away and wriggled back.
And here the grottoes of the trout
Were searched and morsels raided out.
Tracks, retraced and blurred, express
His ritual of cleanliness;
With etiquette of innate laws
He gripped each bit in eager paws
And washed it, feasting all alone.
Then here beside a moss-grown stone
He paused, content with his repast.
He left his signature at last
In ink of night, and he was gone,
His page concluded with the dawn.

—GERTRUDE RYDER BENNETT

---

1. One of the ways of describing things is to compare them to something else: "She is a rose garden." "He is a wolf."

Consider the first line of the above poem. The strip of sand beside the brook is compared to a book, and written upon its pages, as if in printed letters, are the paw marks of a raccoon. You could examine these paw marks and tell what the raccoon had been doing, just as you could read the printed letters in someone's diary and learn his activities.

This comparison of one thing to another is called a "metaphor."

Think of someone eating breakfast. Describe, in metaphors, the food he ate and the way he ate it.

2. There is another way of describing things by comparison, called a "simile." A simile is a metaphor which uses "like" or "as" to make the comparison: "Mr. Harrington came to the breakfast table as cross as a bear." The simile can be turned into a metaphor when a writer wishes to to make his comparison in a less direct fashion: "Mr. Harrington lumbered into the kitchen, growled at the children, and stuffed a piece of toast into his mouth."

In a few paragraphs, describe something or someone—serious or funny—using both similes and metaphors.

3. The author of this poem describes a fact about raccoons that we find interesting and amusing: "With etiquette of innate laws/He gripped each bit in eager paws/And washed it, . . ." All raccoons wash their food before eating. No mother raccoon teaches her offspring to do this; it is an "innate law"—an instinctive action.

Think back to your earliest memories. Can you remember anything you did—or didn't do—simply by following your own instinct? Describe your thoughts and actions in a page or so. If your memory fails, describe a childhood action you think may be instinctive.

NATURE

CIVILIZATION IS IN DANGER of being churned up in the wheels of its own machinery. Whether at work or play we have become dependent on machines. We think in terms of machines, when we think at all, because we have lost touch with Nature through the distractions of town life and the pursuit of false gods.   —W. P. PYCRAFT, from *The Courtship of Animals*

---

1. "Civilization is in danger of being churned up in the wheels of its own machinery."
Pycraft wrote this sentence more than fifty years ago. When we read it today, perhaps we agree with him, perhaps not. After all, jet planes pour tons of kerosene smoke into the air. And yet, a computer, in one minute, can do a job which would take a man one hundred years.
In a page or so, write the how and why of your opinion of the first sentence of the above passage.

2. Pycraft says that the distractions of town life and the pursuit of false gods have caused us to lose touch with nature. In a few paragraphs tell some of the distractions of town life which *appeal* to you.

3. In your opinion, has the machine called education caused us to lose touch with nature? If you think it has, say how you feel nature might be brought back into the schools. If you think it has not, tell several ways you feel that our schools might be improved.

4. In a few paragraphs, tell of some of the "false gods" which you, or someone you know, have pursued.

A CHIRPING CRICKET holds his wings over his back, slanting up at an angle of about 45 degrees, and rubs their bases together vigorously. Each species has its more or less characteristic note and sequence. Some of our pale, greenish-white tree crickets of the genus *Oecanthus* are particularly sensitive to the temperature of the environment while chirping, speeding up as the temperature rises. So accurately are they adjusted that the temperature in degrees Fahrenheit can be calculated quite accurately by counting the number of chirps in fifteen seconds and adding 39. Or you may multiply the temperature by four and subtract 160 to predict the number of chirps per minute. Try it some summer evening—but make sure that you are listening to a tree cricket!

—ALEXANDER and ELSIE KLOTS, from *Living Insects of the World*

1. This really works! Try it and see!

More amazing, perhaps, than the fact that it works is that somebody found out about it.

In a page or so, describe the sort of person who would have the idea of comparing the fluctuations of cricket chirps to the fluctuations of a thermometer.

2. There is a superstition that a cricket is happy, and also that it brings good luck.

In a few paragraphs, speculate as to why this should be.

3. In a page or so, tell about someone whom you feel deserves the nickname "Cricket."

A SNAKE CHARMER or fakir at work may be interesting to watch, but he does not actually charm the snakes, and many of his actions are for the benefit of his audience rather than the snakes. The eerie squeaky music he produces is a total loss as far as the snakes are concerned, for they are stone deaf. They are, however, very sensitive to any vibrations which pass through the ground or the basket in which they are kept. By surreptitiously tapping the basket or stamping on the ground, supposedly keeping time to the music, the fakir can induce the snakes to rear. As he plays his instrument, he keeps his body in constant motion, and the "dancing" or swaying of the snakes is the result of his movements. A cobra whose body is raised in striking position follows the object of its attention; as the fakir moves about, the snake also moves its body to keep its eyes continuously fixed upon the snake charmer.

—OSMOND P. BRELAND, from *Animal Life and Lore*

---

1. We've all of us seen, either in the flesh, or on the screen, or bursting out of the TV, these snake-charming fellows, tootling a woodwind until up from the basket comes the cobra and begins to "dance." Now we learn that . . . we learn that . . .

In a few paragraphs, say what it is that we learn.

2. Tell, in a page or so, of a person you know who pretended to be doing something, but really wasn't doing it at all.

3. You were asked to put on a fifteen-minute entertainment at a school assembly. On the spur of the moment, you agreed. After the spur of the moment had gone, you realized that you didn't have the slightest idea what to do. But it was too late, you'd agreed, and would have to go through with it.

In a page or so, tell one of two things: (a) the thought sequence during which you decided what to do, or (b) the fifteen minutes of your school assembly entertainment.

cities

The ULTIMATE PROBLEM is money—or rather, the problem of not enough money. Whatever else a city can do, it cannot provide the services its people want if it does not have the money to pay for them. And our cities don't have the money. There is no other business I can think of where the proprietor knows *absolutely* that he will face bankruptcy every year. Yet my own city's expenses—with no increase at all in programs—go up each year three times as much as revenues. That does not make for tranquillity. It does make for citizens who must wonder every year whether their local library will cut back its hours, whether their children will be forced to attend split sessions in the schools, whether their hospital can be modernized to meet inevitably higher demands.

—JOHN V. LINDSAY, from *The City*

1. Who'd want to be the mayor of a large city, as was John V. Lindsay when he wrote this book! The problems are endless. Solve one and two more pop up. It reminds you of the legendary monster, the Hydra, which had nine heads, and which the Greek demigod Hercules confronted. Hercules's task was to cut off all its heads. But a problem arose. Every time he cut one off, two grew in its place. He finally solved the problem. He took along a companion who stood by with a flaming torch. Hercules cut off a head, and immediately his companion burned its roots.

In a page or so, tell of a problem which you've confronted in which troubles increased rather than decreased. Or you may write about an acquaintance, or a fictitious character instead.

2. John Lindsay says that "the ultimate problem is money." How true! Once someone, with great excitement, said that he had found something that could be used instead of money. Unfortunately, he went away before he said what it was.

For a page or so, be this "someone" just spoken of. But this time, stay and tell about the "something" that could be used instead of money.

3. As Lindsay says so mournfully, prices are going up and up, and it becomes more difficult to maintain the same standard of living.

In a few paragraphs, tell (mournfully, if you wish) the effects upon your life of the sky-high rising of prices.

65

A CITY, unless it has ceased to have other functions than to serve the purposes of archeology, is always in transition. So long as people live in it and use it, a city can never be completed in the sense that a picture, a statue or a building can be completed. Because of this, there can be no final, once-and-for-all answer to the city's problems. The goal is always advancing, constantly shifting and altering, and usually enlarging.

—MILES J. COLEAN, from *Renewing Our Cities*

---

1. Picture for yourself the city which has ceased to have other functions than to serve the purpose of archeology. Let the picture slide from a city to a person who has ceased . . .

Now, with this person (real or fictional) well in mind, write a page or so of description.

2. It's a fine idea that "so long as people live in it and use it, a city can never be completed."

In a few paragraphs, say whether you have the same feeling about the place (city, town, village, or otherwise) where you live.

3. There is an old saying: "You can't spit in the same stream twice." As a matter of fact, the ancient Greeks went so far as to say: "You can't spit in the same stream once."

In a page or so, tell of an experience you have had that illustrates the idea of everything or everyone continually changing.

THE AUTOMOBILE HAS not merely taken over the street, it has dissolved the living tissue of the city. Its appetite for space is absolutely insatiable; moving and parked, it devours urban land, leaving the buildings as mere islands of habitable space in a sea of dangerous and ugly traffic. . . . Gas-filled, noisy and hazardous, our streets have become the most inhumane landscape in the world.

—JAMES MARSTON FITCH, from *The New York Times*

1. What is this automobile, that it should push us around so ruthlessly? We take it on the chin, we humans, even assisting in our own demolishment.

Two people have a vigorous conversation. One says that the automobile must be stopped before it destroys us. The other says: "Ridiculous! The automobile is too important, and must be given every encouragement."

In a page or so, reproduce that conversation.

2. It is a fact of evolution that the species which survived over the millions of years were the ones which successfully adapted themselves to the difficulties of the surrounding environment.

In a page or so, describe a race of humans who have successfully adapted themselves to the difficulties introduced by the automobile. (Say there were many who did not adapt successfully, were not able to reproduce their kind, and thus were not the ancestors of the present-day population of automobile-escapers.)

3. In a few paragraphs, describe the thing in your life (automobiles excepted) which you consider most detrimental to your hope for peaceful and happy progress.

CITIES

WHY DON'T WE get on with the job of making our great cities efficient and livable and noble? Are we short of labor? Are we short of steel, cement, aluminum, glass? Are we short of architects and engineers? Not for a minute. They are all waiting to be utilized, waiting to make their contribution. What we are short of is organized management, the right governmental setup, practical dreams, and the drive to go ahead together. And yet, these are precisely the qualities that made America great! —LUTHER HALSEY GULICK, from *The Metropolitan Problem and American Ideas*

---

1. The questions asked in the above passage are known as "rhetorical" questions. They are asked more to tell you something than to elicit information.

For instance: you are confronted by a friend who says to you, "Lend me a buck 'til tomorrow?" You reply, "What's the matter, are you crazy?"

In several paragraphs, set up several situations and ask several rhetorical questions.

2. You are given the task of making your school more "efficient, livable, and noble." In a page or so tell, first, what there is about your school which needs to be made more "efficient, livable, and noble," and, second, how you will go about it.

If it should be that your school does not need to be made more "efficient, livable, and noble," do the same thing for a place which needs that treatment.

3. Tell, in a few paragraphs, what needs to be done to you by yourself in order to change yourself into the sort of person who has qualities you would consider admirable in someone else.

CITIES

JUST BY WAY of anticlimax, I might say that my brother, Ernie, who did not heed the advice to go to the *big* city and get a *big* job with a *big* salary, stayed at home. He eventually became mayor, head of a business, and bank president, and is more successful financially than I ever hope to be. He knew that opportunity is where you are. Most people are still chasing rainbows. —H. CLAY TATE, from *Building a Better Town*

---

1. There's an old story of a man who was looking for mushrooms. He had to have some mushrooms! (This was in those backward days before grocery stores offered them in all sizes, shapes, and forms.)

So he set forth upon his search. Month after month he traveled, mile after mile. Finally he returned home, discouraged, sick at heart, still aching for mushrooms.

And what did he see, growing in his own front yard? Mushrooms!

In a page or so, write a similar experience had by you, a friend of yours, or some creature of your imagination.

2. In a page or so, give your opinion of the relative values of living in either large cities or small towns.

3. There's the saying that it's better to be a big frog in a little puddle than a little frog in a big puddle.

In a few paragraphs, describe one of each.

CITIES

Where are the majestic cities of yesteryear?

There was Babylon, so splendid that it was called "The Gate of the Gods," so large that according to Herodotus, its protective walls, set in an exact square, were each fourteen miles in length—a city easily capable of two million or more inhabitants based on today's densities. Yet Babylon was reduced to rubble as a result of the fortunes of war.

Where is Carthage?—A city known for its commercial and military harbors, the granary of the ancient Mediterranean world, with flourishing industry and mining and with, at its peak, a population of perhaps a million people. Carthage, too, was utterly wrecked by the vengeful Romans who had sworn its destruction. —OSCAR STEINER, from *Downtown U.S.A.*

---

1. And our cities will also, someday, be gone. There is no doubt at all, if we can make predictions based upon the experiences of the past.

Maybe not. It's possible, of course, that they'll remain.

But, for this moment, let us assume that our cities will also, someday, be gone.

In a page or so, speculate upon the causes of the passing away of our cities.

2. In a few paragraphs, outline a story in which something you have loved is beginning to slowly disappear as you watch it, helpless to stop its disappearance.

3. Write concerning the things in your life which you hope will be permanent.

POLLUTION

1.

If you visit American city,
You will find it very pretty.
Just two things of which you must beware:
Don't drink the water and don't breathe the air.
—TOM LEHRER, from "Pollution"

1. You are spending your vacation in a spot far away from home. You've met someone you like, and hope that person will visit you.

You are describing your home town. Suddenly you realize that there are a few things in your home town that are rather unpleasant, but in all honesty you should tell about them, the bad as well as the good.

In a page or so, do just that.

2. Have you ever met anyone with *no faults at all?* If you have, describe this person. If not, describe the faults with which you can most easily live.

3. Perhaps the complete elimination of pollution from our land is an impossible dream. In a few paragraphs, tell about a task you've been given which is really impossible to complete, no matter how hard you work on it.

2.

THEN A STRANGE BLIGHT crept over the area and everything began to change. Some evil spell had settled on the community: mysterious maladies swept the flocks of chickens; the cattle and sheep sickened and died. Everywhere was a shadow of death. The farmers spoke of much illness among their families. In the town the doctors had become more and more puzzled by new kinds of sickness appearing among their patients. There had been several sudden and unexplained deaths, not only among adults but even among children, who would be stricken suddenly while at play and die within a few hours.

There was a strange stillness. The birds, for example—where had they gone? Many people spoke of them, puzzled and disturbed. The feeding stations in the backyards were deserted. The few birds seen anywhere were moribund; they trembled violently and could not fly. It was a spring without voices. On the mornings that had once throbbed with the dawn chorus of robins, catbirds, doves, jays, wrens, and scores of other bird voices there was now no sound; only silence lay over the fields and woods and marsh.

On the farms the hens brooded, but no chicks hatched. The farmers complained that they were unable to raise any pigs—the litters were small and the young survived only a few days. The apple trees were coming into bloom but no bees droned among the blossoms, so there was no pollination and there would be no fruit.

The roadsides, once so attractive, were now lined with browned and withered vegetation as though swept by fire. These, too, were silent, deserted by all living things. Even the streams were now lifeless. Anglers no longer visited them, for all the fish had died.

In the gutters under the eaves and between the shingles of the roofs, a white granular powder still showed a few patches; some weeks before it had fallen like snow upon the roofs and the lawns, the fields and streams.

No witchcraft, no enemy action had silenced the rebirth of new life in this stricken world. The people had done it themselves.

This town does not actually exist, but it might easily have a thousand counterparts in America or elsewhere in the world. I know of no community that has experienced all the misfortunes I describe. Yet every one of these disasters has actually happened somewhere, and many real communities have already suffered a substantial number of them. A grim specter has crept upon us almost unnoticed, and this imagined tragedy may easily become a stark reality we all shall know.

—RACHEL CARSON, from *Silent Spring*

---

1. In the second line of the above passage is the phrase "evil spell." In a paragraph or so, describe the perpetrator of this "evil spell."

2. Things that have not happened but might happen are often more terrible than those which have already taken place. Have you ever lived through any such experience? If so, tell about it at length. If not, imagine such a situation and tell about it at length.

74

W<small>HATEVER A HONEYMOON VISIT</small> to Niagara Falls was like in the days when Blondin was crossing on his tightwire, it's different now. Something new and unpleasant has been added. Sightseers boarding the famous *Maid of the Mist* excursion boat are likely to find themselves shrouded in a miasma that smells like sewage. That's what it is—coming over the American falls in the Niagara River and gushing out of a great eight-foot culvert beneath the Honeymoon Bridge. As the little boat plows through the swirling currents to a landing on the Canadian side, it has to navigate an expanse of viscous brown foam—paper-mill waste out of the culvert— that collects in a huge eddy across the river.

—<small>GLADWIN HILL</small>, from "The Great and Dirty Lakes"

---

1. Like Abou Ben Adhem in the poem by the same name by Leigh Hunt, you love your fellow men. But you also love the beautiful woods across the road from the house in which you live.

One morning you are awakened by a great clatter. Bulldozers, axes, chain saws have begun to work in the woods. They are clearing the land. One hundred houses will be built. No woods anymore. A housing development.

In a page or so, describe your thoughts as you watch the bulldozers, axes, chain saws.

2. You are the president of the paper mill mentioned in the above passage. Your secretary brings you the morning mail. One of the letters is from a honeymooner, telling you in rather forceful terms that your mill—with its wastes—spoiled his honeymoon excursion.

You decide to answer his letter. In a few paragraphs, do so.

T<small>ODAY'S POPULATION IS</small> about eight times that of 1850 but produces thirty-five times as much. In putting forth this great rise in material goods it also produces, as a by-product, thirty-five times as much noise. And whereas in 1850 only 15 percent of the people were submitted to production's bang-and-clatter, today 70 percent of the people are so afflicted. Nor is this development peculiar in the United States; it is an international problem of the whole capitalistic and communistic world.

Something is going to have to give. In the category of aspirin we have the ear plugs and ear mufflers advised by an airfield official, the thick acoustical ceilings and sound-proof-vault houses advised by a building contractor, the double-paned windows advised by a glass manufacturer, the heavy insulated draperies and heavier carpets, the sheets of gypsum and acoustical tiles advised by the appropriate commercial proponents.

—ROBERT RIENOW and LEONA TRAIN RIENOW, from *Moment in the Sun*

---

1. One of the dangerous forms of pollution of our day is noise pollution. There are all sorts of frightening statistics to indicate its force. But most of us don't need statistics to tell us how fiercely the noises assail us.

We have invented all kinds of "sound-proofing" devices, yet the problem is still with us. Suppose that nature will come to our "rescue." In a page, tell how the problem of noise pollution might be solved by nature. Before you begin writing, consider the possibility that nature's "solution" might create an even more serious problem.

2. Say all you wish, then picture (with your inward eyes and ears) a rock band in full production. In a few paragraphs, say why this is hugely enjoyable, but the sounds of jet planes horrendous.

3. You are the director of a large airport. You have been receiving letters, phone calls, threats of all sorts from people who live nearby. No sleep night or day, they say, no nerves unfrazzled, not even the ability to think about how much they hate you.

You prepare a letter in answer. In a page or so, write that letter.

■ POLLUTION ■

THE AFFLUENT SOCIETY is based partly upon the discovery that it is cheaper to produce something in quantity than to repair it. If the automobile part and its installation cost $6.24, and the mechanic's time to repair it would cost $7.14, obviously you are better off to get a new part. There is a slight fallacy, in that no one considers what happens to the old part. It is dumped somewhere, of course, and these thousands and thousands of discarded gadgets come to form a part of the engulfing mass.

—GEORGE R. STEWART, from *Not So Rich as You Think*

---

1. Each time you buy something new and throw the old thing away, the heaps of junk in our world grow higher.

Now, when you toss a piece of junk out of your car onto the road, or into a field, or somewhere other than a litter bag or a garbage can, you're making the land that much less beautiful. It used to be that after a while the unbeautiful bit of junk would rot away or dissolve. But not so with much of our modern junk. Plastic—it doesn't rust, or dissolve. It stays there. Tin cans which used to rust away in a few weeks—nowadays they're specially treated with chemicals which keep them from rusting for a long, long time.

So, our very smartness, our technical know-how, is one of the greatest "uglifiers" of our world.

In a page or two, tell about some junk you've been accumulating along the path of your recent travels.

2. Speaking of junk: one of the greatest problems is the disposal of old cars. In a few paragraphs, write what you think of the present system of old car disposal.

3. To continue with the matter of old cars: you have an old car. It's arrived at the point where it is completely kaput.

There is no automobile junkyard within fifteen miles of your kaput car. In a few paragraphs, say what you will do with your car.

SURVIVAL

THE WHOLE PROCESS of spraying seems caught up in an endless spiral. Since DDT was released for civilian use, a process of escalation has been going on in which ever more toxic materials must be found. This has happened because insects, in a triumphant vindication of Darwin's principle of the survival of the fittest, have evolved super races immune to the particular insecticide used, hence a deadlier one has always to be developed—and then a deadlier one than that. It has happened also because, for reasons to be described later, destructive insects often undergo a "flare-back," or resurgence, after spraying, in numbers greater than before. Thus the chemical war is never won, and all life is caught in its violent crossfire.

—RACHEL CARSON, from *Silent Spring*

1. Many things that man has made, which at first seemed to benefit him, have turned out to harm him. In a few paragraphs, tell about something that you once did for someone which you thought would help but which turned out to be anything but a help.

2. In the first line of the above passage Rachel Carson speaks of "an endless spiral." She refers, of course, to the process of spraying insects with chemicals.

In a few paragraphs, tell about something in your exeperience which has been caught up in "an endless spiral."

3. Miss Carson says that because of chemical sprays, insects have evolved super races immune to the particular insecticide used. She says that this is an example of Darwin's principle of the survival of the fittest.

Suppose you sprayed 100 insects with a killing chemical. Ninety-nine of them die. These 99 were not fit, they would not survive to reproduce themselves.

But one insect does not die. She is fit. She is able to survive this poison. She will mate and produce offspring which will inherit her ability to resist this killing chemical. She will reproduce, let us say, 1,000 offspring, 250 of which will inherit her ability to resist the killing chemical. These 250 will be fit; they will survive. They will reproduce themselves and pass on to their offspring this ability.

Imagine a human situation in which the weakest have succumbed and the strongest have survived. Write about it.

4. Because of this development of super races of insects, says Miss Carson, "the chemical war is never won and all life is caught up in its violent crossfire."

In a few paragraphs, paint a word picture of this "crossfire."

SURVIVAL

I MUST CONCLUDE these notes about sleep by relating a very curious case of sleep, resembling the winter-sleep of higher animals, on the part of a snail. This was the case of a desert snail from Egypt, which was withdrawn into its shell, the mouth of the shell being closed with a glistening film secreted by the snail, as is usual with snails in this country in winter when they sleep. The desert snail in question was affixed to a tablet of wood in a glass case in the natural history department of the British Museum on March 25, 1846. On March 7, 1850, that is four years afterward, it was noticed by a visitor looking at the case that the snail had emerged from his shell and discolored the paper around, but had again retired. So the officials unlocked the case and removed the snail from the tablet and placed him in tepid water. He rapidly and completely recovered, crawled about as a wide-awake snail should, and sat for his portrait. This may be regarded as an instance of unusually long sleep, natural to this species of snail, and related probably to the frequently prolonged dryness of the snail's surroundings.

—SIR RAY LANKESTER, from *Science From an Easy Chair*

---

1. The ability to "turn yourself off" is, at times, extremely valuable. Surely you must know someone who makes you long for the condition of the snail described above when it is your unfortunate lot to be around him.

In a page or so, tell of an evening spent in the presence of that person.

2. There must be things upon this earth which especially bore you, or especially delight you. In a few paragraphs, tell about some of them.

3. In a page or so, tell about the person with whom you'd most prefer to spend five years on a desert island.

F EAR of what we do not know or do not understand has been with us in all ages. Man, knowing that his life will end, has often been prey to an even more terrible nightmare—the end of his whole world. In a scientific age most of the past terrors have turned out to be senseless chimeras. But one menace remains. It is the great and permanent unknown: what will we humans do to each other and to ourselves?

—EDWARD TELLER and ALBERT L. LATTER, from *Our Nuclear Future*

1. Scientists frequently ask themselves whether or not they should investigate everything, whether or not there are some subjects they should leave alone.

You are a scientist, and have just made a discovery. At first you are tremendously elated. But then you begin to think about things, and suddenly your elation turns to terrible despair.

In a page or so, tell about your discovery, and the reason your elation turned to despair.

2. The authors of the above passage speak of "past terrors" which have turned out to be "senseless chimeras." A chimera, according to *Webster's New Collegiate Dictionary*, is "a frightful, vain, or foolish fancy."

In a page or so, tell about a terror, real or fictitious, which turned out to be a senseless chimera.

3. Regard the last sentence of the above passage. In a few paragraphs, comment upon it.

H E BEGAN TO ACCOMPANY his mother on the meat trail, and he saw much of the killing of meat and began to play his part in it. And in his own dim way he learned the law of meat. There were two kinds of life— his own kind and the other kind. His own kind included his mother and himself. The other kind included all live things that moved. But the other kind was divided. One portion was that his own kind killed and ate. This portion was composed of the nonkillers and the small killers. The other portion killed and ate his own kind, or was killed and eaten by his own kind. And out of this classification arose the law. The aim of life was meat. Life itself was meat. Life lived on life. There were the eaters and the eaten. The law was: EAT OR BE EATEN.

—JACK LONDON, from *White Fang*

---

1. "He" in the above passage, as you probably know, is a young wolf.

Jack London, author of the passage, says that there is a law which governs the lives of wolves: "Eat or be eaten."

In other words, "law" isn't limited to a group of rules set up by a group of men, and administered by a group of law enforcement officers. Law can be something else, too.

In a page or so, describe this other kind of law in your own life.

2. You are a young anteater, frisking through the South American jungle with your mother.

She teaches you some manners. In a page or so, say what manners she taught you, and how she went about it.

3. In the above passage, London describes the awakening to the law by a young wolf beginning to hunt for food.

In the same manner as that used by London, describe the awakening to the law by a child beginning to go to kindergarten.

SURVIVAL

W HEN MAN THINKS of his own age he is often inclined to look enviously at animals which are supposed to attain a particularly great age. But not all the stories about centuries-old parrots and ancient elephants and crocodiles are true. Most land mammals do not attain a great age. Horses seldom reach 40, wild boars and red deer live to about 30, cattle to 25, dogs to 15, rats and mice about three years. With the big beasts of prey it is easy to miscalculate: lions and tigers seldom live for more than 20 years and the wolf's maximum is 15. On the other hand, elephants can live to a great age; one has been kept in captivity for 120 years. Some of the cold-blooded vertebrates are long-lived, too. The crocodile, like the toad, lives only to the age of 40, but it is known that giant tortoises can reach the age of 300 years and more. Frogs and salamanders do not live for much longer than ten years. Even among the invertebrates there are some surprising figures: a North American cicada needs 17 years to develop fully, and many queen ants live to 12 or 15. The bird spider of South America is supposed to live for ten years, and it is said that the earthworm can reach the same age. On the other hand, flies live only for one or two months; the *Ephemeridae* often no more than a day.

—FRITZ-MARTIN ENGEL, from *Life Around Us*

1. Have you ever looked enviously at an animal, as Fritz-Martin Engel says you might have looked? Engel adds that the look of envy is due to your belief that the animal is going to live a great deal longer than you.

But there may be other areas of envy than age.

In a page or so, contrast some of the major qualities of animals and man, pausing now and then to say whether there is anything to be envied.

2. There has been much study among animal psychologists (men and women who study the psychology of animals) as to which animal is the brightest and which is the dullest.

You must have formed some ideas concerning these matters. In a page or so, make a statement concerning the type of animal you consider to have the highest I.Q., and proceed to tell why.

3. Think of that elephant, mentioned in the above passage, who had been in captivity for 120 years! Put yourself in its place. Give some of the thoughts which would have passed through your head during those 120 years.

SURVIVAL

THE COCKROACH IS UNHONORED and unsung. It walks about with downcast eyes. Its head hangs dejectedly between its knees. It lives on modest fare and in humble circumstances. It is drab-colored and inconspicuous. But don't let that Uriah Heep exterior fool you. For here you have Superbug, himself!

During 100,000,000 years, the cockroach has been a winner. Dinosaurs sent roaches scuttling up the trunks of prehistoric trees; but roaches lived to see these monsters disappear forever. Before any bee or ant or butterfly appeared, cockroaches were holding their own, as they are today. Wherever food and warmth are found, there is a cockroach also. One species even lives so far north it dines on dried fish in the huts of the Laplanders.

If an inventor sat up nights trying to devise an indestructible bug, he would have a hard time outdoing the roach. Its seed-shaped body is smooth and waxed, as hard to hold as a slippery orange-pip. Its flat form permits it to squeeze into incredibly small cracks. Its nimble legs provide such speed and shiftiness that it could give pointers on openfield running to an All-American halfback. Delicate body hairs catch vibrations and warn of approaching danger and its long, slender antennae form a super-sensitive nose for smelling hidden food. Its body is a living thermometer, reacting quickly to any changes in temperature and enabling it to select living quarters where the average warmth is between seventy and eighty degrees F. Break off a cockroach's leg and, if the insect has not reached its full size, another grows in its place. By sleeping daytimes and coming abroad at night, the roach avoids most of its natural enemies. So sensitive is its body to light and shade that a completely blinded cockroach will infallibly seek the dark.

In addition, a roach seems to have an internal anatomy as immune to stomach ache as a concrete-mixer. Its jaws will tackle whitewash, grease, hair, paint, honey, beer, bedbugs, gold lettering on books, and watercolor paints as readily as they will meat and potatoes. A cockroach is an insect goat with a goat's appetite raised to the Nth power. Moreover, its body requires so little oxygen that it can live for hours after all its breathing tubes have been sealed with paraffin. Roaches get along with about half as much blood, in relation to body weight, as humans require. Nitrogen is needed in the diet of other forms of life, but none is required by the adult cockroach.   —EDWIN WAY TEALE, from *Adventures in Nature*

If you knew someone who had even half the ability that the cockroach has to survive the difficulties, the entanglements, the dangers, the messes, and the muddles of living, you would probably admire him or her no end. How unfair we are to "Superbug"!

Perhaps you know someone (a human being) who has some amazing qualities. (Don't ever tell him that he reminds you of a cockroach.)

In a page or so, describe this someone and his amazing qualities.

If you don't know such a person, create one.

86

beauty

Li Fu-jen

The sound of her silk skirt has stopped.
On the marble pavement dust grows.
Her empty room is cold and still.
Fallen leaves are piled against the doors.

Longing for that lovely lady
How can I bring my aching heart to rest?

—WU-TI

1. We read the above poem, written by Wu-ti, Emperor of China from 140 to 87 B.C., and we are overtaken by a sense of grief for the loss, not only of "that lovely lady," but for the "lovely lady" whom we ourselves shall some day lose. We sense, also, that grief is a part of life, as joy is a part of life.

In a page or so, tell of a grief that you have had.

2. In a few paragraphs, describe the emotion of happiness.

3. Bertrand Russell, the philosopher, wrote: "Whatever can be *known* can be known by science."

In a few paragraphs, give your opinion as to why Mr. Russell placed the word "known" in italics the first time.

K INSEY WAS a short, slender individual, who was inordinately proud of his clothes. He kept himself tailored to the minute, and had his hair trimmed every third day. His nails were glistening, his hands were as soft as his eyes were hard.

As someone had expressed it, Kinsey was always trying to improve the appearance of the package, because he knew that the goods inside were rotten.

—ERLE STANLEY GARDNER, from *The Case of the Screaming Woman*

1. Where have you come across a person similar to Kinsey, described in the above passage? In a page or so, describe this person, and give your opinion of him.

2. In an act of imagination (perhaps loathsome to yourself), become an evil-thinking-and-acting person who wishes his victims to believe he is kindly-thinking-and-acting.

You are getting ready to move in on a new victim. In a page or so, tell about the preparations you make.

3. In a few paragraphs, describe the early days which would turn a person into the sort you have imagined yourself to be in the question above.

BEAUTY

God's World

O world, I cannot hold thee close enough!
 Thy winds, thy wide gray skies!
 Thy mists, that roll and rise!
 Thy woods, this autumn day, that ache and sag
 And all but cry with color! That gaunt crag
 To crush! To lift the lean of that black bluff!
 World, World, I cannot get thee close enough!

Long have I known a glory in it all,
 But never knew I this:
 Here such a passion is
 As stretcheth me apart—Lord, I do fear
 Thou'st made the world too beautiful this year;
 My soul is all but out of me—let fall
 No burning leaf; prithee, let no bird call.

—EDNA ST. VINCENT MILLAY

---

1. Poets are enthusiastic people. What love Miss Millay has, what ecstasy, on this day she tells about in the above poem.

Sometime, surely, during your complicated life, you've had a day, or a moment, which you remember with great joy. In a page or so, tell about it. On the off chance you've never had one, make up a little story about a day, or a moment of great joy in the life of your favorite fictitious character.

2. Time and civilization move on. Say that the state plans to build a superhighway right across a place you love dearly. Therefore, that place will be gone forever.

Someone says, "Write a letter to the Commissioner of the State Highway Department, urging him to change the direction of the superhighway so the place will not be destroyed."

You decide to do so.

Write that letter.

3. When a place or a thing is owned by someone, its use can be forbidden, by law, to anyone but the owner.

Are there any places or things which you feel should not be owned by anyone at all?

In a page or so, say what they are, and why you feel no private ownership of that place or thing should be allowed.

BEAUTY

WHAT MAKES A WOMAN BEAUTIFUL in a man's eyes? Warm red lips or a pale, uncolored mouth? A fluff of short, soft curls or a sweep of long, straight hair? A reed-slim shape or gently rounded curves? Pretty, healthy pink cheeks or a smooth, creamy complexion?

Obviously, each man's ideal differs somewhat from every other man's. But we have long suspected that certain vogues in beauty change not merely with the centuries but with the decades, and that men as little as ten years apart in age may have quite different ideas of what constitutes a really good-looking woman.   —from *McCall's*

1. Concerning the question raised in the first sentence of the above passage: it could also read, "What makes a man handsome in a woman's eyes?"

The writer of this passage seems to think that tastes vary. In a page or so, set down your ideal of beauty in the opposite sex.

2. You are a parent. Your fifteen-year-old child asks you a question: "What is the most important quality of love?"

In a page or so, answer your child.

3. There's an old song: "Will you love me in December as you did in May?" In the lyrics which follow, there are certain answers given.

But, we do not have the lyrics. You be the lyricist of the song, and write a few paragraphs telling how your feelings toward a loved one might be affected during the long years.

BEAUTY

O beautiful for spacious skies,
For amber waves of grain,
For purple mountain majesties
Above the fruited plain!

America! America!
God shed His grace on thee
And crown thy good with brotherhood
From sea to shining sea!
—KATHERINE LEE BATES,
from "America the Beautiful"

1. Perhaps it seems odd to think of it this way, but one of our dearest personal possessions is our country. And also, one of the most beautiful things we know is our country.

And that is one of the reasons why it hurts so to see pollution increasing, or violent dissension separating men.

In a page or so, give your ideas along these lines.

2. In a page or so, describe something (not someone) you've seen in this country which you feel is particularly beautiful and particularly "yours."

3. Suppose you're an astronaut. A year ago you landed on a distant planet, where the living is good. A few months ago something happened to your spaceship, and now it is broken beyond repair, and you can't use it to return to Earth. The planet you're on has not yet developed spaceships, and you personally haven't the ability to build one.

Every evening you sit and watch Earth come up over the horizon. In a page or so tell your thoughts as you watch.

health

Fortunately, most of the diets described in health books are so weird that people won't follow them for long. But there are always exceptions. In New York, a young woman recently starved herself to death on the Zen Macrobiotic diet, which is popular among hippies. A hardback book called *Zen Macrobiotic Diet* sells well on health food book racks, and a health food supermarket in Manhattan offers weekly cooking classes in Zen Macrobiotic foods. Briefly, MB, as its adherents call it, involves seven levels of progressively more severe diets, the last of which consists solely of brown rice. Every mouthful of food must be chewed at least 50 times as fluid intake is strictly limited. Such a dietary regime will produce spiritual enlightenment, as well as ward off old age and illness, says its founder, Japanese author George Ohsawa. MB dieters seem to agree with him. "I've never felt better," observed one Harvard student. "My asthma has cleared up, my headaches are gone, my back has stopped aching, and I need two hours less sleep a night." Another Harvard MB man reported that "your mind escapes from your body."

Dr. Stare sees MB differently. "Macrobiotic effects," he says, "have nothing to do with the magical properties of brown rice. They are simply symptoms of mild starvation accentuated by psychological suggestion."

—BARBARA O'CONNELL, from "The Wacky World of Food Fads"

---

1. The ancient philosophers known as Epicureans used to cry out: "Let us eat, drink, and be merry, for tomorrow we die!"

Now, many people bent upon losing weight cry out, "Let us eat, drink, and be merry, for tomorrow we diet."

Surely you've known someone bent upon losing weight. Perhaps you've even entertained the idea yourself. In a page or so, drawing upon your observations or personal recollections, speak of this outcry of dieters-to-be.

2. In a few paragraphs, say why the sort of activity described by Barbara O'Connell in the above passage should be known as "food faddism."

3. The whole thing ceases to be amusing when you think that a very high percentage of the people in the world—men, women, and children—are of necessity on a starvation diet. Each day they eat even less than the starved young woman mentioned in the above passage.

In a page or so, give some practical suggestions for enabling these many starvation-diet people to enlarge their daily consumption of food.

Aмerican children are the least physically fit children in the world today. And this is not the moment in history when we can afford to bear such a distinction. It isn't good for the children, it isn't good for the family, and it certainly isn't good for the nation.

It would be very comforting if we could prove the above statement false, but that has been tried and it didn't work. The original study on *minimum* muscular fitness in school children here and in other countries was made with a medically valid test. In 1955 the findings were presented to President Eisenhower at a meeting in the White House and from that meeting came the President's Council on Youth Fitness.

Since that time, many other tests have been used, but the original findings still stand. Physically, we don't compare well with other countries. We don't even compare well with the last generation of Americans.
—BONNIE PRUDDEN, from "A Formula for Family Fitness"

1. It seems as if we'll have to take Bonnie Prudden's word for the amazing first sentence in the above passage.
In a few paragraphs, try to account for this depressing fact.

2. Each spring physical fitness tests are given at every school. In a page or so, tell about a strange, humorous, or peculiarly interesting performance that you have witnessed, or in which you have taken part.

3. In a page or so, tell of an experience you have had, or have witnessed, in which physical fitness played the major role.

Many of the effects of inhaling cigarette smoke are similar to the effects of breathing highly polluted air. People install air conditioners in their homes and places of work, or travel out of the cities, to get away from polluted air. Yet, curiously, many of them continue voluntarily to inhale the most intensely polluted air to which man is exposed.
—HAROLD S. DIEHL, M.D., from *Tobacco and You*

1. It's bad enough to be slowly poisoned by the careless actions of other people. But to slowly poison yourself! This seems the greatest folly.

And yet it goes on. Millions of people keep right on puffing along. They don't care, they don't believe it can happen to them, they can't kick the habit. Mostly the latter.

But when young people, just coming up, get the habit, it's nothing less than tragic.

In a page or so, tell about someone you know who tried to kick the habit, successfully or unsuccessfully. And if you don't know anyone—well, you know what to do.

2. In the above passage Dr. Diehl comments that people buy air conditioners or travel away from the city to get away from polluted air. And polluted it is! Not only in cities, but in small towns too!

In a page or so, describe the most air-polluted place you know.

3. Let's get back to smoking.

You are a small brother or a small sister. Your big brother or big sister catches you smoking. In a page or so, reproduce the conversation that ensues.

HEALTH

THOSE APPLES you bought at the supermarket for the children's lunch today—you made sure they were red, succulent, unblemished. But did you suspect they were probably shot through from peel to core with some of the most powerful poisons known?

And how about that prepared cake mix for tonight's dessert? Does it contain real eggs and shortening, or were these replaced by an inexpensive chemical that offers no nutritional value and has caused extensive organic damage and even death to laboratory animals?

—WILLIAM LONGGOOD, from *The Poisons in Your Food*

---

1. The first paragraph of the above passage sounds like a paragraph from a tale of terror and cruelty. But, of course, it isn't.

We make a lot of poisons in our chemical factories, and we use them to get rid of insects and other pestiferous creatures. And sometimes we get rid of creatures which we never intended to destroy.

97

In a page or so, tell how you, or someone you know, once ate, by mistake, something that did you no good.

2. In a paragraph or so, give your opinions concerning the use by farmers and gardeners of chemical pesticides.

3. In a few paragraphs, give your viewpoint concerning synthetic foods, or food additives, used for aesthetic reasons only (for instance, chemicals to make white bread whiter or oranges more orange).

HEALTH

MANY PARENTS also commit a grievous error that actually encourages their child to eat aspirin tablets. They tell him that the aspirin is candy to get him to take it without a fuss. It's all done with the best of intentions and in the interests of expediency, but this little white lie is exceedingly treacherous. Dr. Roger J. Meyer, now on the staff of the University of Vermont Medical School, did a comprehensive analysis of 94 aspirin poisoning episodes. There were 84 instances in which candy aspirin was incriminated. In *all but one* of these instances, the parents of the poisoned child admitted telling him it was candy! —JEAN CARPER, from *Stay Alive!*

---

1. Many parents have a strange hang-up. They feel that they have to protect their children from all things which may be even a little unpleasant. And so, out of what they consider to be the "goodness of their hearts," they lie to their children.

Think back over your lifetime. Can you remember any situation in which your parents, or anyone else, deceived you, hoping to make things easier for you? Write, in a page or so, the results of your thinking. If thinking back brings no memory, construct one.

2. Some years back, someone wrote a play entitled: "Another Language." The idea behind it was that no matter how close we are to each other, none of us really talks the same language.

In a few paragraphs, give your opinion about this "another language" idea.

3. In half of a page or so, reproduce the conversation you might have had with a person of your acquaintance, trying to convince him that it would be a great pleasure for him to lend you a dollar.

IDENTITY

Love

O My Luve's Like a Red, Red Rose

O my Luve's like a red, red rose
    That's newly sprung in June:
O my Luve's like the melodie
    That's sweetly played in tune.

As fair art thou, my bonnie lass,
    So deep in luve am I;
And I will luve thee still, my dear,
    Till a' the seas gang dry:

Till a' the seas gang dry, my dear,
    And the rocks melt wi' the sun;
I will luve thee still, my dear,
    While the sands o' life shall run.

And fare thee weel, my only Luve!
    And fare thee weel awhile!
And I will come again, my Luve,
    Tho' it were ten thousand mile.
               —ROBERT BURNS

---

1. Poets often seem to have stronger feelings than other men. Robert Burns, who wrote the above poem, must have felt very strongly about his "luve" to write about her as he did.

In a page or so, and with the enthusiasm of Robert Burns, describe your sweetheart, or the sweetheart of anyone you might know or imagine.

2. Shakespeare asked, "Whoever lov'd that loved not at first sight?"

In a few pages, say whether or not you believe in love at first sight, and, if you do, describe your or someone else's falling in love at first sight. If you don't believe in it, give the sequence of falling in love.

3. In a few paragraphs, say whether or not you think it is possible to love anything nonhuman (a dog, a cat, a bird, a horse, a fish, a hamster, an automobile, a pair of skis, a gun, a yo-yo) as much as a human being.

103

On the Death of Smet-Smet, the Hippopotamus-Goddess

SONG OF A TRIBE OF THE ANCIENT EGYPTIANS

(*The Priests within the Temple*)
SHE was wrinkled and huge and hideous? She was our Mother.
She was lustful and lewd?—but a God; we had none other.
In the day She was hidden and dumb, but at nightfall moaned in the shade;
We shuddered and gave Her Her will in the darkness; we were afraid.

(*The People without*)
　　She sent us pain,
　　　　And we bowed before Her;
　　She smiled again
　　　　And bade us adore Her.
　　She solaced our woe
　　　　And soothed our sighing;
　　And what shall we do
　　　　Now God is dying?

(*The Priests within*)
She was hungry and ate our children;—how should we stay Her?
She took our young men and our maidens;—ours to obey Her.
We were loathèd and mocked and reviled of all nations; that was our pride.
She fed us, protected us, loved us, and killed us; now She has died.

(*The People without*)
　　She was so strong;
　　　　But death is stronger.
　　She ruled us long;
　　　　But Time is longer.
　　She solaced our woe
　　　　And soothed our sighing;
　　And what shall we do
　　　　Now God is dying?

—RUPERT BROOKE

104

1. In some ancient religions, it seems, God could die, and often did so. And this is the setting of the above poem—God is dying.

In a page or so, write the ideas which the poem arouses in you.

2. "She sent us pain,/ And we bowed before Her;/ . . . She solaced our woe and soothed our sighing;/"

No doubt about it, we can forgive cruelty in a person if he also brings us comfort.

Write a few paragraphs describing someone in your life who combined these qualities. If there was no one in your life who brought to you these qualities, write of an imaginary relationship of this type.

3. Suppose you were a priest, or a priestess, of Smet-Smet, and your duty is to speak to the people and bring them comfort, as their god is dying.

(Suppose it this way: a friend of yours is dying and you must bring comfort to other friends.)

What would you say to them?

LOVE

When you were a Tadpole and I was a Fish,
In the Paleozoic time,
And side by side on the ebbing tide,
We sprawled through the ooze and slime,
Or skittered with many a caudal flip
Through the depths of the Cambrian fen—
My heart was rife with the joy of life,
For I loved you even then.
                    —LANGDON SMITH, from "Evolution"

---

1. You say to your sweetheart: "I will love you forever!" That takes care of the future. But do you also say, "I have loved you always," as Langdon Smith says in the poem above?

In a page or so, tell about time spent with your sweetheart in an age now gone. You have no sweetheart? Imagine one!

2. There is an old saying: "First love is best love." How about that? In a few paragraphs give your opinion of this old saying.

3. "My heart was rife with the joy of life." There are those who claim that being in love brings a new exhilaration to all areas of living. In a few paragraphs, say what you think of those who make this claim. You have never been in love? Then say, in a few paragraphs, why you would, or would not, wish to be in love.

LOVE

IF I WERE TO DIE tomorrow, I would tell you this tonight: I love you. These are easy words to say, yet my heart fails as I say them, for their meaning is as full and musical as the Bell of Doom. Men are such fools that they have but one name for a thousand meanings, and beggar the poor love word to base kitchen usages and work-a-day desires. But I would keep it holy for the flame which it sometimes pleases heaven to light in one heart for the worship of another. I never knew what love was till I saw a girl's face on a May morning and wisdom stripped the rind from my naked heart. The God in me leaped into being to greet the God in your eyes. I love you. This is what I would say if I were to die tomorrow."

He was very close to her now, and his eyes were looking into her eyes. She answered him frankly:

"If you were to die tomorrow, I might tell you this much tonight. A woman may love a man because he is brave, or because he is comely, or because he is wise, or gentle—for a thousand thousand reasons. But the best of all reasons for a woman loving a man is just because she loves him, without rhyme and without reason, because heaven wills it, because earth fulfills it, because his hand is of the right size to hold her heart in its hollow."

—JUSTIN HUNTLY MC CARTHY, from *If I Were King*

---

1. The above passage is from a play which was enormously popular during the early years of this century. The man is going into battle the next day. He knows it is possible that he may be killed.

He mentions one of the sad lacks of the English language (and there is the same lack in many languages): we use the word "love" to convey many meanings. And yet there is, really, a considerable difference in personal feeling between "I love her," and "I love her gooseberry pie," or "I love him," and "I love the way he handles a car."

Write a page or so, which shows a conversation between you and your loved one, in which you distinguish clearly between the various shades of meaning of the word "love."

2. In a page or so, tell about a time when you were watching someone standing there, and suddenly your world changed. If this never happened to you, write a little story about its happening to a character in your imagination.

LOVE

Gone

Everybody loved Chick Lorimer in our town
       Far off.
       Everybody loved her.

So we all love a wild girl keeping a hold
       On a dream she wants.
Nobody knows now where Chick Lorimer went.
Nobody knows why she packed her trunk . . . a few old things
And is gone,
       Gone with her little chin
       Thrust ahead of her
       And her soft hair blowing careless
       From under a wide hat,
Dancer, singer, a laughing passionate lover.

Were there ten men or a hundred hunting Chick?
Were there five men or fifty with aching hearts?
       Everybody loved Chick Lorimer.
       Nobody knows where she's gone.

                 —CARL SANDBURG

1. Surely, Chick Lorimer, in the above poem, reminds you of someone you have come across during your lifetime. Not the same, but someone like her.

In a page or so, describe this person.

2. Something about Chick Lorimer, as Carl Sandburg describes her, made it inevitable that she leave "our town / Far off." Restlessness? What?

Let us pretend that Chick Lorimer left a letter, saying why she was leaving. In a page or so, write that letter.

3. Regard line 4 in the above poem. Sandburg says: "So we all love a wild girl keeping a hold on a dream she wants."

In a few paragraphs, say whether or not you agree with Sandburg, and why.

LOVE

The Little Bird

One morning I got up
to pick oranges in the garden.
And I saw this.
I saw the rising sun
and the little bird
singing his morning song.
And I heard this.
The little bird chirped: "Cui, cui, cui!"
And begged:
"Please, leave my little ones in their nest."
And I said this:
First I chirped: "Cui, cui, cui!"
And then I said:
"Don't be afraid, I am your friend."
And what was asked I did.

Since that day the little bird loves me
and his sweet song gives me great pleasure.
And this is what happened.
—GABON FOLK SONG

1. This is a folk song from Gabon, on the coast of West Africa.
No doubt about it, the person in the poem has a great feeling of fellow-ship with the little bird.

Have you ever had such a feeling for an animal? If not, have you ever known anyone who did? If not, surely you can imagine someone having one.

Write a page or so telling about that feeling.

2. The bird (mother or father) had a great fear: that the man would take its little ones from the nest.

For a page or so, be a mother, or a father (bird or human). You have a fear similar to the bird in the poem. Tell about this fear.

3. What a lovely ending the poem has! The man and the bird are friends now. So the bird sings sweetly to the man, and the man does not frighten the bird.

In a page or so, tell your ideas of true friendship.

FEAR

THE VOICE OF THE OLD MAN with the long white beard, the only occupant of the carriage with him, broke sharply in like a steel knife cutting through blotting paper.

"Pardon me, but there is a spider on your neck!"

Harkness started up. The two books slipped to the floor. He passed his hand, damp with the afternoon warmth, over his cool neck. He hated spiders. He shivered. His fingers were on the thing. With a shudder he flung it out of the window.

—HUGH WALPOLE, from *Portrait of a Man With Red Hair*

1. The spider in the above passage was only doing its thing. It probably had no intention whatsoever of biting or in any other way harming the neck or any other part of Mr. Harkness. Yet Mr. Harkness shivered, shuddered, grasped the spider, and threw it out of the window.

Who feels sorry for the spider? Do you? If so, say, in a few paragraphs, why you feel sorry. If you don't, say, in a few paragraphs, why you don't feel sorry.

2. There is a saying that if you step on a spider, there will be rain on that day.

Maybe you believe this or maybe not. But, some people would *never* step on a spider, especially if they hadn't brought their raincoats.

In a page or so, give your opinion of superstitions in general. Whether or not you have a particular opinion, tell about a few superstitions.

3. In a page or so, tell how you, or someone of your acquaintance, avoided a great peril.

ONCE LONG AGO as a child I can remember removing the cover from an old well. I was alone at the time and I can still anticipate, with a slight crawling of my scalp, the sight I inadvertently saw as I peered over the brink and followed a shaft of sunlight many feet down into the darkness. It touched, just touched in passing, a rusty pipe which projected across the well space some twenty feet above the water. And there, secretive as that very underground whose mystery had lured me into this adventure, I saw, passing surely and unhurriedly into the darkness, a spidery thing of hair and many legs. I set the rotting cover of boards back into place with a shiver, but that unidentifiable creature of the well has stayed with me to this day.

For the first time I must have realized, I think, the frightening diversity of the living; something that did not love the sun was down there, something that could walk through total darkness upon slender footholds over evil waters, something that had come down there by preference from above.   —LOREN EISELEY, from *The Immense Journey*

---

1. The "spidery thing of hair and many legs" mentioned above preferred the dark sliminess of the depths of a well to the daylight of the world outside.

Do you know anyone who prefers "darkness" to "light"? If so, write a page or so describe him. If not, construct someone of this sort.

2. How strange it seems that we really know nothing at all of the ideas and fancies that tick through the other fellow's head.

In a page or so, tell how the same essential idea might run through: (a) your mind, and (b) another person's mind. To begin, invent an imaginary situation involving you and someone else.

3. In a few paragraphs, say what there is about a spider that causes a feeling of horror in most people.

FEAR

"LEAVE ME NOW," said a stern voice behind him.

He turned and hurried out, just conscious that the dead man had been thrust back into the chair, and that Campbell was gazing into a glistening yellow face. As he was going downstairs he heard the key being turned in the lock.

It was long after seven when Campbell came back into the library. He was pale, but absolutely calm. "I have done what you asked me to do," he muttered. "And now, good-by. Let us never see each other again."

"You have saved me from ruin, Alan. I cannot forget that," said Dorian, simply.

As soon as Campbell had left, he went upstairs. There was a horrible smell of nitric acid in the room. But the thing that had been sitting at the table was gone.   —OSCAR WILDE, from *The Picture of Dorian Gray*

---

1. This passage, like nearly all the passages in this book, is "out of context." In other words, you don't know what precedes or what follows the passage.

In a paragraph or so, say what you think might have been the reason that "He" (who "turned and hurried out") asked Campbell to do a particular job for him.

2. "And now, good-by. Let us never see each other again."

There must be someone of your acquaintance to whom you would be glad to say these two sentences. Tell about him (or her).

If there is no one to whom you would be glad to say those words, tell about a person, who is not yet of your acquaintance, to whom you would like to say, "Hello! Let us see each other again and again!"

3. If your reading and reacting to the above passage have aroused in you any particular emotion, write what that emotion is, and try to account for it. Don't forget: No reaction at all is an emotion—call it "a feeling of nothingness." So, if the above passage leaves you with a feeling of nothingness, tell what there is about the passage, or about you at this particular moment, that has led to this result.

4. Campbell, in the above passage, seems to be a rather intriguing person, who did a certain deed, and remained "pale but absolutely calm." Write a few hundred words, fictitious or factual, telling how you, or a person known to you, did a certain deed and remained ——— but ———.

===== FEAR =====

I̲t walked in the woods.

It was never born. It existed. Under the pine needles the fires burn, deep and smokeless in the mold. In heat and in darkness and decay there is growth. There is life and there is growth. It grew, but it was not alive. It walked unbreathing through the woods, and thought and saw and was hideous and strong, and it was not born and it did not live. It grew and moved about without living.

It crawled out of the darkness and hot damp mold into the cool of a morning. It was huge. It was lumped and crusted with its own hateful substances, and pieces of it dropped off as it went its way, dropped off and lay writhing, and stilled, and sank putrescent into the forest loam.

It had no mercy, no laughter, no beauty. It had strength and great intelligence. And—perhaps it could not be destroyed. It crawled out of its mound in the wood and lay pulsing in the sunlight for a long moment. Patches of it shone wetly in the golden glow, parts of it were nubbled and flaked. And whose dead bones had given it the form of a man?

It scrabbled painfully with its half-formed hands, beating the ground and the bole of a tree. It rolled and lifted itself up on its crumbling elbows, and it tore up a great handful of herbs and shredded them against its chest, and it paused and gazed at the gray-green juices with intelligent calm. It wavered to its feet, and seized a young sapling and destroyed it, folding the slender trunk back on itself again and again, watching attentively the useless, fibered splinters. And it snatched up a fear-frozen field-creature, crushing it slowly, letting blood and pulpy flesh and fur ooze from between its fingers, run down and rot on the forearms.

It began searching.   —THEODORE STURGEON, from "It"

---

1. We know that this creature, "It," who is the hero of the above passage, must have existed, because Theodore Sturgeon has described it. We also know (at least we hope) that "It" existed only in Sturgeon's mind.

Can something, or someone, really exist only in your mind? Something very real to you, but only to you? Write a few paragraphs giving your answer to this question.

2. Make a huge effort and become "It." You were never born, yet you exist. You have no mercy, no laughter, no beauty. You scrabble painfully with half-formed hands.

What do you think about? Put down your thoughts in a page or so.

3. You are in the woods, gathering wild flowers, or tracking a small animal, and are suddenly confronted with "It." In a few hundred words, tell what would be your reactions—physical, mental, and spiritual—to this confrontation.

Then, without any warning, a Silver Man came out of a recess behind the image of the god. He was perfectly naked in that bitter, bitter cold, and his body shone like frosted silver, for he was what the Bible calls "a leper as white as snow." Also he had no face, because he was a leper of some years' standing and his disease was heavy upon him. We two stooped to haul Fleete up, and the temple was filling and filling with folk who seemed to spring from the earth, when the Silver Man ran in under our arms, making a noise exactly like the mewing of an otter, caught Fleete around the body, and dropped his head on Fleete's breast before we could wrench him away. Then he retired to a corner and sat mewing while the crowd blocked all the doors.

—RUDYARD KIPLING, from "The Mark of the Beast"

1. Tell about the ideas and images that came to you as you read the above passage. Imagine you were present when the leper appeared, and describe your reactions in a page or so.

2. Many readers say that they find in Kipling's writings a sort of eerie quality, which gives them the feeling of being in a world rather different from their everyday world. If you are affected in this way by the above passage, say what it is in the writing which gives you this feeling. If not, write a few paragraphs which will convey an "other world" feeling.

3. The first sentence of the above passage mentions "the image of the god." This refers to the statue of a Hindu god in a temple in India. The "Silver Man" has been standing behind the statue.

Here we have something terrible in appearance (the Silver Man) concealed behind something beautiful and highly inspiring (the image of the god). The two, seen together, make a rather affecting contrast: fright and high inspiration.

Write a paragraph or so, fictitious or factual, in which there is a similarly strong contrast.

4. Because of the terror which a leper aroused, he was an extremely lonely person.

For the moment, you are a leper, watching a group of people recoiling from you in horror. In a few hundred words, tell about the effect this has upon you.

aloneness

THE WHOLE SCHOOL RUSHED noisily into the playground. The new boys were told to go into the middle, while the others stationed themselves along opposite walls. They began to play *Pig in the Middle*. The old boys ran from wall to wall while the new boys tried to catch them: when one was seized and the mystic words said—one, two, three, and a pig for me— he became a prisoner and, turning sides, helped to catch those who were still free. Philip saw a boy running past and tried to catch him, but his limp gave him no chance; and the runners, taking their opportunity, made straight for the ground he covered. Then one of them had the brilliant idea of imitating Philip's clumsy run. Other boys saw it and began to laugh; then they all copied the first; and they ran round Philip, limping grotesquely, screaming in their treble voices with shrill laughter. They lost their heads with the delight of their new amusement, and choked with helpless merriment. One of them tripped Philip up and he fell, heavily as he always fell, and cut his knee. They laughed all the louder when he got up. A boy pushed him from behind, and he would have fallen again if another had not caught him. The game was forgotten in the entertainment of Philip's deformity. One of them invented an odd, rolling limp that struck the rest as supremely ridiculous, and several of the boys lay down on the ground and rolled about in laughter: Philip was completely scared. He could not make out why they were laughing at him. His heart beat so that he could hardly breathe, and he was more frightened than he had ever been in his life. He stood still stupidly while the boys ran round him, mimicking and laughing; they shouted to him to try and catch them; but he did not move. He did not want them to see him run any more. He was using all his strength to prevent himself from crying.

—W. SOMERSET MAUGHAM, from *Of Human Bondage*

1. In a page or so, tell about an adventure you have witnessed similar to the one described in the above passage.

2. You are the parent of Philip in the above passage. When he limps home from school with a tear-stained face and torn, dirty clothes, he tells you about his adventure. Following this, you and he have a conversation.

In a page or so, recount that conversation.

IN THE BEGINNING the solitude was painful except when a gale was blowing to keep him busy. He fell into the habit of giving commands and answering them. When he was in his cabin, having lashed the rudder, he yelled every once in a while to an imaginary hand at the helm: "How does she there?" Then he would answer: "All right, sir; all right, sir!" At the meridian altitude of the sun he would call aloud: "Eight bells!" The sense of loneliness passed, but he continued to shout commands and answer himself respectfully. —PETER FREUCHEN, from *Book of the Seven Seas*

1. The character in the above passage was Joshua Slocum, the first man to sail around the world alone. On July 1, 1895, when he set out from Yarmouth, he was fifty-one years old. His ship was an old sloop.

He returned to Newport July 3, 1898.

In a page or so, describe this man, and say something of his life previous to July 1, 1895.

2. You are in prison. Four days ago they put you in solitary confinement for five days.

In a page or so, say why you were sent to prison, why you were given five days in solitary, and what you intend to do tomorrow when your five days are up.

3. Did you ever hear anyone talking to himself, either sleeping or waking? If so, describe, in a few paragraphs, his conversation. If you never heard such a thing, manufacture that incident.

An Epitaph

Here lies a most beautiful lady,
Light of step and heart was she;
I think she was the most beautiful lady
That ever was in the West Country.

But beauty vanishes; beauty passes;
However rare—rare it be;
And when I crumble, who will remember
This lady of the West Country?

—WALTER DE LA MARE

---

1. This poem is said by its author to be engraved upon a tombstone near a small church in southwestern England, "the West Country."

In a page or so, tell the story of the "most beautiful lady" who lies buried.

2. How quickly human beings—living, breathing, laughing, suffering individuals—are forgotten when they are no longer with the people among whom they once lived.

In a page or so, write about someone you once knew, but now know no more. If such a person is not in your experience, imagine one to write about.

3. Is there a "most beautiful lady," or a "most wonderful man" in your life? If so, tell about her or him. If not, imagine someone you'd like there to be.

ALONENESS

Is THIS, THEN, all that life amounts to—to stumble, almost by mistake, into a universe which was clearly not designed for life, and which, to all appearances, is either totally indifferent or definitely hostile to it, to stay clinging on to a fragment of a grain of sand until we are frozen off, to strut our tiny hour on our tiny stage with the knowledge that our aspirations are all doomed to final frustration, and that our achievements must perish with our race, leaving the universe as though we had never been?   —SIR JAMES JEANS, from *The Mysterious Universe*

---

1. You have just read the above passage, and are lost in thought. You feel a slight poke in the ribs. It is the person sitting next to you, who points out that you've been asked a question three times, and that the entire class is waiting for you to respond.

For a moment your mind is bouncing back and forth between infinity and your desk in a rather small classroom.

In a few paragraphs, tell what goes on in your mind as it bounces back and forth.

2. Someone said to you: "I am the most important person in the entire world."

Your first reaction is that this person must be some sort of schizophrenic or something. (You've always thought of him as a pipsqueak.)

But you begin to rethink. The result of your rethinking is that he is absolutely correct. He *is* the most important person in the entire world.

In a page or so, set down the course of thinking which brought you to the conclusion that he was correct. (If, after having considered the matter as generously as you can you still think he's a schizophrenic, set *that* down, of course.)

3. In a page or so, say whether or not, in your opinion, the universe will continue after all life has ceased to exist.

■■■■■■■■■■■■■■■■■■ A L O N E N E S S ■■■■■■■■■■■■■■■■■■

The White Dress

Some evening when you are sitting alone,
   by your high window, motionless and white—
I shall come, by the way that none but I have known,
   into the quiet room out of the night.

You will know I have come, without turning your head
   because of the way the air will lie quite still,
as though it waited for something to be said
   that no man has ever said, and no man will.

But you will be wiser than the air. You know
   that for the thing we feel there is no word—
and you will not move even when I turn to go,
   even when the sound of my footsteps is no longer heard.
                —HUMBERT WOLFE

1. In a page or so, say what thoughts ran through your mind while you were reading the above poem.

2. When there is love between two people, sights unseeable, sounds unhearable, words unsayable sometimes pass between them—whether or not they are both present.

If you have experienced this, tell of your experience. If you've never experienced it, construct a scene between two people of your imagination.

3. The above poem is a fantasy. The poet, and the reader too, know that this could not really happen.

In a series of paragraphs, construct several fantasies—events that could not happen in actuality.

4. Have a go at speculating why Humbert Wolfe, author of the above poem, entitled it "The White Dress." In a paragraph, set down your speculations.

ALONENESS

Eleanor Rigby

I look at all the lonely people
I look at all the lonely people
Eleanor Rigby picks up the rice
in a church
where a wedding has been
Lives in a dream
Waits at the window, wearing the face
that she keeps
in a jar by the door
Who is it for?

All the lonely people
where do they all come from?
All the lonely people
where do they all belong?

Father McKenzie, writing the words
of a sermon that no one will hear

No one comes near
Look at him working
darning his socks in the night
when there's nobody there
What does he care?

All the lonely people
where do they all come from?
All the lonely people
where do they all belong?

I look at all the lonely people
I look at all the lonely people

Eleanor Rigby died in the church
and was buried along with her name
Nobody came
Father McKenzie, wiping the dirt
from his hands
as he walks from the grave
No one was saved

All the lonely people
where do they all come from?
All the lonely people
where do they all belong?
  —JOHN LENNON and PAUL MC CARTNEY

---

  1. The writers of this song must have had a great curiosity about their fellow men, and also a great understanding of them.
  Look around you, meditatively, in the classroom. Then write a page or so in the manner of the above passage (prose or verse), and speak of some of those people whom you see.

  2. The word "lonely" is continuously used in the above passage. Just what is "loneliness"? What does it mean, "a lonely person"? In a few paragraphs, give your meaning.

  3. Some people seem to fear solitude more than others. In a page or so, say how you react to solitude, and give an example or so to illustrate your reaction.

Individualism

Africa's Plea

I am not you—
but you will not
give me a chance,
will not let me be *me*.

"If I were you"—
but you know
I am not you,
yet you will not
let me be *me*.

You meddle, interfere
in my affairs
as if they were yours
and you were me.

You are unfair, unwise,
foolish to think
that I can be you,
talk, act
and think like you.

God made me *me*.
He made you *you*.
For God's sake
Let me be *me*.

—ROLAND TOMBEKAI DEMPSTER

---

1. In this poem, Roland Tombekai Dempster makes Africa speak. But we might well imagine that he himself is speaking. Or, that it might be anyone who wishes to be left alone to be himself.

In a page or so tell of someone in your acquaintance who would like to be left alone to be himself.

2. How often an autobiography, written by a ninth- or a tenth-grader, begins: "Oh, I'm just the same as everybody else, I guess."

What is your opinion of the above statement? Do you think that any one person can be exactly like any other one person?

3. And yet there's no doubt about it. People certainly try to be like other people. In fashions, for instance. In 1948 dresses *had to be exactly* four inches off the floor. In 1968 dresses *had to be exactly* six inches above the knee.

In a page or so give your explanation of the fact that there is a part of us that wishes to conform, and a part that wishes to be individualistic.

INDIVIDUALISM

Society everywhere is in conspiracy against the manhood of every one of its members. Society is a joint-stock company, in which the members agree, for the better securing of his bread to each shareholder, to surrender the liberty and culture of the eater. The virtue in most request is conformity. Self-reliance is its aversion. It loves not realities and creators, but names and customs.

Whoso would be a man, must be a nonconformist. He who would gather immortal palms must not be hindered by the name of goodness, but must explore if it be goodness. Nothing is at last sacred but the integrity of your own mind.   —RALPH WALDO EMERSON, from "Self-Reliance"

---

self-reliance: individualism
conformity: doing what the Establishment (society) says to do
joint-stock company: a big business corporation
aversion: extreme dislike

---

1. Here is one of America's most respected philosophers saying that the most precious possession of each one of us is our individualism. Here he is saying that society, sometimes known as the Establishment, tries very hard to rob each one of us of our individualism.

In a few paragraphs, say whether or not you think this attempt at thievery is a good or a bad thing.

2. What do you think of people who scorn other people because their ideas are different? Describe such a person in a page or so and include your reactions to that person.

3. Reread the above passage. Consider the first sentence of the last paragraph. Write a half page or so in comment upon it.

Consider the last sentence of the passage. Write a half page or so in comment upon it.

INDIVIDUALISM

My Beard

IS IT STRANGE IS IT FRIGHTENING TO SEE
DOES IT DERANGE OR BRING CHANGE
TO YOUR RULES OF CONFORMITY?

Why do you frown at my beard—
An item so dear to me?
Does it bring to mind
That I'm trying to find
A thing you may never see—
A thing from the past
To which I hold fast
Known as identity?

—JIMMIE SHERMAN

1. Among the blindest people in the world are those who gaze upon another person and do not see him. Not the real person. These people don't see, and they don't even try to see. They don't want to see.

In a page or so, tell about someone you know who resents, resists, and reprimands you or someone of your acquaintance for being a little different from him.

131

2. What do any of us have which is *really* ours?

In a page or so, say what, in your opinion, you have that is *really* yours.

3. In the world of today it is possible to observe many styles of dress or appearance of people who are "doing their thing."

In a page or so, describe a person you've seen whom you consider to have departed farthest from the conventional.

■■■■■■■■■■ INDIVIDUALISM ■■■■■■■■■

The Road Not Taken

Two roads diverged in a yellow wood,
And sorry I could not travel both
And be one traveler, long I stood
And looked down one as far as I could
To where it bent in the undergrowth;

Then took the other, as just as fair,
And having perhaps the better claim,
Because it was grassy and wanted wear;
Though as for that, the passing there
Had worn them really about the same,

And both that morning equally lay
In leaves no step had trodden black.
Oh, I kept the first for another day!
Yet knowing how way leads on to way,
I doubted if I should ever come back.

I shall be telling this with a sigh
Somewhere ages and ages hence:
Two roads diverged in a wood, and I—
I took the one less traveled by,
And that has made all the difference.

—ROBERT FROST

1. The speaker of this poem seems to be telling the story of a youthful decision he made, and its meaning in his life. While you are reading it, you are aware that this adventure is something that probably happens, in one form or another, in everyone's life.

In a page or so, tell of such an adventure in your life. If you can't think of one, tell of someone you know.

2. There is a poem by the American poet John Greenleaf Whittier entitled "Maud Muller." It tells of a man and woman who might have, but did not marry, and how both sorrowed over the years because they had not taken this step.

Toward the end of the poem occur the two lines:
"For of all sad words of tongue or pen,
The saddest are these: 'It might have been!' "
In a few paragraphs, outline a story to illustrate these two lines.

3. Write a paragraph or so of your explanation of the last two lines of Frost's poem.

INDIVIDUALISM

I AM NOT one of those who, seeing a rainstorm on a summer's day, think only of the ravaged crops, and the ruined peasants. . . . I am one of those who think: So much the better; the weather will be cooler and it will be good to breathe; I love the air when it has been swept by rain. . . . I do not consider anything but my pleasure: I accept my own being; I am the Egotist; I am Myself.

—STENDHAL, from *Recollections*

1. The world is made up of many kinds of people. Write three, six, or nine paragraphs, one third of them telling the kind of person you are, one third of them telling the kind of person you would like to be, one third telling the kind of person that other people would like you to be.

2. Among the people you know, can you point out any who fit the description given in the above passage: "who, seeing a rainstorm on a summer's day, think only of the ravaged crops, and the ruined peasants"? The description of such a person will surely take at least a page.

3. Among the people you know, can you point out any who fit the passage's description: "I am one of those who think [concerning the rainstorm on a summer's day]: So much the better; . . . I love the air when it has been swept by rain."

Description of such a person will surely need a page.

4. What about the person who does not consider anything but his own pleasure, who is an egotist, who is himself? What do you think of this sort of person? Describe such a person—or imagine one—in two or three paragraphs.

youth

The Oldest April

It is always so—
When the world is tip-toe at the edge of spring,
When there is this wide, incredible morning sky
And air touches the cheek like a woman's hand,
Then are the small and secret-meaning songs
That children make blown through my heart again;
Songs that they make of dandelions and dew
And hum softly, having no words,
Knowing no name for beauty.

So it is—always.
When I feel the dark earth turning in its sleep
Or hear a bird cry out with a sudden call
I remember the oldest April;
Thinking of a peeled sapling switch with the grace of a girl
And the feel of a pebble I once closed into my hand
And a plum tree that I knew that bloomed one night
And trembled standing between me and the moon.
For each of these there is a song I made
Long ago on the green hill of childhood.
Only for the plum tree I made no song
Because it was too beautiful.
Even in a child's heart it is like that.

—SARAH LITSEY

1. In a page or so, say what ideas run through your mind as you read this poem.

2. Each day that takes us further away from our childhood may cause us to forget it more and more. We can lose the knowledge of past extreme delights and sadnesses.

For a few moments return to your childhood and write about a great joy or a great sadness that you had.

3. There is so much imagination in children's play, so much that comes unchanged from their hearts. As they become older, this spontaneity changes.

In a page or so, say what, in your opinion, happens to this spontaneity.

YOUTH

A LOT OF THE TIME we are very unhappy, and we try to cheer ourselves up by thinking. We think how lucky we are to be able to go to school, to have nice clothes and fine things and to eat well and have money and be healthy. How lucky we are really. But we remain unhappy. Then we attack ourselves for self-pity, and become more unhappy, and still more unhappy over being sad.

We're unhappy because of the war, and because of poverty and the hopelessness of politics, but also because we sometimes get put down by girls or boys, as the case may be, or feel lonely and alone and lost.
—JAMES SIMON KUNEN, from *The Strawberry Statement*

1. The more we learn of the world in which we live, the more we are aware of the needs and denials, the hopes and the disappointments, the sweet and the bitter. As our education progresses, we become more and more "citizens of the world."

And often, as in the case of James Kunen, author of the above passage, we are overtaken by *weltschmerz. Weltschmerz* is a German word meaning "a sense of the sadness of the world."

In a page or so, tell about your *weltschmerz.* If you have none, tell about your sense of the joy of the world.

2. You go over to visit your friend at his house, and find that he is in a state of unhappiness bordering upon utter despair.

In a page or so, tell how you attempt (successfully or not) to cheer him up.

3. In a few paragraphs, explain the clause in the next to last line of the above passage: "get put down by girls or boys."

When I Was One-and-Twenty

When I was one-and-twenty
   I heard a wise man say,
"Give crowns and pounds and guineas
   But not your heart away;
Give pearls away and rubies
   But keep your fancy free."
But I was one-and-twenty,
   No use to talk to me.

When I was one-and-twenty
   I heard him say again,
"The heart out of the bosom
   Was never given in vain;
'Tis paid with sighs a-plenty
   And sold for endless rue."
And I am two-and-twenty,
   And oh, 'tis true, 'tis true.

—A. E. HOUSMAN

1. Perhaps this poem will make some people angry: it doesn't speak too highly of falling in love.

However, the poem does make one thing clear: sometimes advice from an older person makes sense. And yet the only thing that most of us learn from is our own experience.

In a page or so, tell about something you, or a person you know, have learned only from experience.

2. What about this poem's attitude toward "giving your heart away"? What are your ideas on the subject? In a few paragraphs, speak!

3. Mark Twain said that when he was seventeen he thought his father was the stupidest man he'd ever met, but when he was twenty-one, he wondered how the old man could have learned so much in four years.

In a page or so, tell about someone in your life who has changed a great deal, or at least has seemed to you to have changed.

Children begin by loving their parents; after a time they judge them; rarely, if ever, do they forgive them.

—OSCAR WILDE, from *A Woman of No Importance*

1. The above passage was written in 1893. It appears in a play by the English writer Oscar Wilde.

Even though it was written seventy-seven years ago, it has a great deal of meaning today. It shows, if nothing else, that some problems are always new and never old.

Take the first part of the statement: "Children begin by loving their parents."

What do your memories bring you concerning this statement? Set them down in a few paragraphs.

2. "After a time they judge them."

Is this true? How exactly do you interpret the two words, "judge them"? A paragraph should be enough.

3. Parents and children suggest "the generation gap." Just what is meant by those three words? In a page or so, give your explanation of the term.

It is bewildering for a parent to watch a pleasant child turn into an unruly teen-ager. Suddenly, nothing suits him. The house is crummy, the car is junky, we are old-fashioned. His inner radar detects what irritates us most. If we value neatness, he will be sloppy. If we insist on good manners, he will interrupt conversations, use profanity and belch in company. If we enjoy language that has grace and nuance, he will speak slang. If we are concerned about health, he will smoke like a chimney and wear summer clothes in freezing weather. Buying a suit, he may ask the salesman, "If my parents like it, can I bring it back?"

—DR. HAIM GINOTT, from *Between Parent and Teen-ager*

1. One's heart certainly bleeds for the poor parents. But how do these bewildered parents think a teen-ager feels? It's extremely weird to be misunderstood by the very ones who should understand you best.

In a page or so, tell the tale of "a pleasant child turning into an unruly teen-ager."

2. In a few paragraphs, tell your favorite age, and why it is your favorite. If you haven't yet reached that age, pretend you've arrived.

3. You are a parent who comes into a room, and finds an unruly teen-ager. Or *vice-versa*. In a page or so, reproduce the conversation that ensues.

YOUTH

THERE HAS NEVER BEEN a generation so detached from their parents. All the practical binds are gone. It has been decades since the average middle-class family needed their adolescent children for anything more than dish-washing, baby-sitting, and lawn-mowing. For the parents, the postwar ties were emotional ones; for the children, the ties were material. Now the children, by rejecting the parents' material values, also throw off the need of support. The society has reached such a point of affluence that a resourceful kid can live off its waste. A kid who lacks resources can live off his peers, who are, more often than not, willing to sustain him. Every commune carries a few.

—DON MC NEILL, from *The Village Voice*

---

1. McNeill says that "it has been decades since the average middle-class family needed their adolescent children for anything more than dish-washing, baby-sitting, and lawn-mowing."

Cast your imagination backward over those decades and be a teen-ager at that time. You are greatly needed by your family.

In a page or so, tell of some of those needs, and of your attitude toward them.

2. McNeill, a little further on, speaks of resourceful kids being able to live off the wastes of society.

141

You are a resourceful kid. Tell about living off the wastes of society. Invent a situation in which you are forced to shift for yourself and describe it in a page or so.

3. In a few paragraphs, outline a speech you are going to deliver to a group of parents, telling them about some of the hang-ups of the times.

━━━━━━━━━ ■ YOUTH ■ ━━━━━━━━━

Aᴛ ᴀ ᴅɪɴɴᴇʀ ᴘᴀʀᴛʏ my husband sat next to a woman who said that her eleven-year-old son was not at all interested in his schoolwork and was just "getting by." She asked my husband what she could do about the situation, and when my husband asked, "What *is* he interested in?" she replied, "His great passion is baseball—but that isn't going to get him into college!" When my husband tried to reassure her that very few eleven-year-olds were normally interested in college, she confessed, "Just the same, every night I go into his room after he's asleep and I whisper, 'I want to be a lawyer, I want to be a lawyer'; it's sort of a homemade 'sleep-suggestion' program." —ᴇᴅᴀ ᴊ. ʟᴇ ꜱʜᴀɴ, from *The Conspiracy Against Childhood*

1. One of the problems with at least some parents is that they get their own ideas all mixed up with their children's ideas, and try to think their children's thoughts for them.

In a page or so, tell of a child who got his parents' ideas all mixed up with his own, and tried to think his parents' thoughts for them.

2. The last sentence of the above passage brings out the phenomenon of "sleep learning." It is supposed to be a fact that you can have a phonograph or a tape recorder near your pillow at night, softly playing the things you want to learn. Next morning you know them!

In a page or so, tell the content of the phonograph record or tape recording you would most like to have playing softly by your pillow at night.

3. About the middle of the above passage occurs the statement: "His great passion is baseball . . ."

In a paragraph or so, tell about a great passion of yours.

142

Sports

I'M A PROFESSIONAL FOOTBALL PLAYER. I joined the Green Bay Packers in 1958, fresh from the University of Idaho, and during my rookie season we were the worst team in pro football. Over the past eight seasons, we've been the best team in pro football. Not coincidentally, our head coach for the past eight seasons has been a man named Vincent Thomas Lombardi, a cruel, kind, tough, gentle, miserable, wonderful man whom I often hate and often love and always respect. I've played next to great football players in Green Bay; sixteen of my teammates have been named to one or another of the All-Pro teams during the past nine years. I managed to make the All-Pro teams four years myself.

Nothing irritates me more than the implication that we're some sort of subhuman beasts, trained animals clawing each other for the amusement of modern Romans. I'm not trying to suggest that pro football players as a group are the intellectual equals of, say, the staff of *The Paris Review*. But I've sat with lawyers and with politicians and with writers, and, frankly, when I want an interesting conversation, I'd just as soon chat with a bunch of pro football players. At least the players are willing to discuss something besides football.

I guess the editor of *The Paris Review*, George Plimpton, feels the same way. He'd rather go to a football training camp than to a literary cocktail party, and I can't blame him.

Not that I have anything against literature, or against cocktails, for that matter. I like to read—poetry, philosophy, novels, almost everything. I don't think my reading habits are exceptional—I certainly don't pretend to be a scholar—but every time a reporter comes to my room in training camp or to my home and sees my books, he seems impressed (The Beast reads!), which makes me suspicious about the reading habits of reporters.

—JERRY KRAMER, from *Instant Replay*

1. Somehow or other, the idea seems to have gotten around that a person who uses his body well can't use his mind well—in other words, that fine athletes are apt to be pretty fine dopes.

This may or may not be true. In your opinion (as expressed by a page or so of writing), support the "may," or the "may not."

2. There is something rather desperate in the first sentence of the second paragraph of the above passage. In a page or so, tell how you felt the time you were completely misunderstood by one or more people.

145

A GREAT BULLFIGHT brings the exaltation great music does and great poetry. One carries for a time afterward the satisfaction and the knowledge that man is no weakling in a dreadful world—that by his bravery, his versatility, and his merits he has and can survive anything the world can bring against him.

That small, unshielded, soft-fleshed, inferior-muscled figure, clad in penetrable silk, armed only with a triangle of woolen cloth and a toothpick of steel can and does face and dominate and kill the reborn force of evil, and fear is the greatest and most poisonous evil we know.

No, I do not love the bullfight, but I love the bull, and I love the man who reassures to us that we are of the race of men.

—JOHN STEINBECK, from "Bullfighting"

1. Surely only a romantic-minded man could feel the exaltation that great music gives while watching a performance about which he says, "No, I do not love the bullfight."

In a page or so, tell of an emotional reaction you have had to some activity you watched or took part in.

2. John Steinbeck, at the end of the second paragraph in the above passage, speaks of fear.

In a page or so, tell how you, or someone you know, have been affected by fear.

3. Describe the type of human being whom you: (a) scorn the most, or (b) admire the most.

GIANTS ARE PEOPLE who do things mortals cannot do, like Goliath on the battlefield. Or like Wilt Chamberlain averaging over 50 points a game one season, leading the pros year after year in scoring and rebounding, making a lion's share of the record book his own. Things like that are merely how a Giant gets to be a Giant—as opposed, say, to the 7-foot freaks who can't play like Wilt and are merely tall. When Wilt does what he does, the fans say, well, what do you expect? And they wait, because sports fans know their fairy tales.

—JEREMY LARNER, from "How Goliath, Typecast to Lose, Finally Didn't"

---

1. One of the finest basketball players of all time, Wilt Chamberlain, is 7 feet, 2 inches tall. He is, thus, a "giant" in two senses: in his physical constitution and in his accomplishments.

You are, during one or more pages, a physical giant. Tell of a day in your life, and some of the problems which arose.

2. In a page or so, describe the giant in accomplishment you would most like to be.

3. In a paragraph or so, think the thoughts you will think when you look, for the first time, upon your first child.

SPORTS

B UT DEMPSEY WAS a picture-book fighter. By all the sons of Mars, he looked the part. He had dark eyes, blue-black hair, and the most beautifully proportioned body ever seen in any ring. He had the wide but sharply sloping shoulders of the puncher, a slim waist, and fine, symmetrical legs. His weaving, shuffling style of approach was drama in itself and suggested the stalking of a jungle animal. He had a smoldering truculence on his face and hatred in his eyes. His gorge lay close to the surface. He was utterly without mercy or pity, asked no quarter, gave none. He would do anything he could get away with, fair or foul, to win. This was definitely a part of the man, but was also a result of his early life and schooling in the hobo jungles, barrooms, and mining camps of the West. Where Dempsey learned to fight, there were no rounds, rest intervals, gloves, referees, or attending seconds. There are no draws and no decisions in rough-and-tumble fighting. You had to win. If you lost, you went to the hospital or to the undertaking parlor. Dempsey, more often than not, in his early days as hobo, saloon bouncer, or roustabout, fought to survive.

—PAUL GALLICO, from "Who Do You Think You Are—Dempsey?"

1. Have you ever seen or known a really tough person? One who, as Dempsey is described in the above passage, is "utterly without mercy or pity, . . . [who] would do anything he could get away with, fair or foul, to win."?

If so, tell about him. If not, construct him.

2. In a page or so, tell of an experience you have had which called for every ounce of your courage and will power.

SPORTS

JOE SUDDENLY STOPPED, peering into the heart of a low-lying shrub. He beckoned to me and I hurried over.

"Look," he said, pointing at the clump.

In its center crouched a small rabbit, motionless except for the vibration of its small nose. It was a shot which would be impossible to miss and I felt secretly envious that I had not been the one to find the bunny. I waited impatiently for Joe to shoot but he remained almost as motionless as the rabbit, watching its big liquid eyes fixed unblinkingly upon us. Then slowly he began to walk toward it. The rabbit waited until he almost stepped on it; then it scrambled away and bounced toward a nearby stone wall. Joe raised his gun quickly and swung it onto the target. But the bang which came a second later exploded from Joe's lips rather than from the gun as the rabbit dove to safety under the wall.

"You didn't shoot!" I gasped.

Joe grinned. "No," he said. "He didn't have a chance. I don't think he'd have tasted very good if I'd shot him like that."

—E. C. JANES, from *A Boy and His Gun*

---

1. In a few paragraphs, give your ideas on hunting as a sport.

2. Sometimes, something happens inside of us, as it did with Joe in the above passage. This something stops us from doing the thing we had intended to do. In your opinion, what is the nature of this something?

3. In the light of your own experience, explain Joe's remarks in the last paragraph of the above passage.

148

FASHIONS

ACTUALLY, I HAD ALWAYS SECRETLY LONGED to wear a beard. I don't know why; perhaps, in childhood, I developed some subconscious Santa Claus fixation. It does not matter, particularly; the point is, I always wondered how I would look behind a beard. But after I made my decision, it took me some time to take the step. A couple of times I left off shaving for three or four days, but my grubby, unkempt chin elicited so many rude and ridiculing remarks—"What's the matter, lose your razor?"—that I could not muster the courage to carry on.

—RICHARD GEHMAN, from "Beards Stage a Comeback"

1. Surely you've had a secret longing for something at some time—perhaps, like the author of the above passage, to learn how your face would appear under different circumstances; or as the result of a particular hair-do, or how your entire self would react to some sort of "new look."

In a page or so, describe your experiences in relationship to your secret longing.

2. In a few paragraphs, say why, in your opinion, Gehman, according to the last clause of the above passage, "could not muster the courage to carry on."

3. Discuss your ideas on the matter of school decisions upon student dress.

FOR THE "SECOND HOME" in the country, paper houses now are available. Combined with aluminum and plastic to make them fireproof and weather-proof, these tentlike dwellings are inexpensive, last an estimated five years and can be collapsed for storage in a garage or cellar.

Paper houses have already been used as dwellings for migratory workers in California. And for furniture: paper chairs and tables are now available in major department stores.

Regardless of the style they choose, it is clear that American families in the days just ahead are to have an increasingly large selection of homes of all types, and they are likely to continue to find a dazzling array of new products with which to furnish them.

—from *U.S. News & World Report* of July 3, 1967

1. It's very swank, having one home in the city, one home in the country. You're a very lucky person.

There's a puzzle here. Everyone knows that people who live in glass houses shouldn't throw stones. But what shouldn't people throw if they live in paper houses?

In a paragraph or so, solve this puzzle.

2. Are people losing weight, and eating lighter food, that they can sit on paper chairs, and eat off paper tables?

In a page or so, tell about an evening spent in your all-paper domicile.

3. Draw on your imagination sufficiently to tell of an evening spent at the domicile into which the paper-house people graduated (to the next building material after paper).

FASHIONS

THE ABILITY TO BELIEVE in magic also kept an estimated 35 million overweight Americans on an all-year hunt for just the right product that would slim them down effortlessly. There was no end to the concoctions and devices they tried out, failed with, and went on to the next. They had available to them bath salts, bath cabinets, and nonporous garments to sweat the fat off. They had soaps, pastes, and creams to wipe it off. They had special girdles and belts to massage it off. They had suction cups designed to pound it off. They had vibratory cushions and chairs to shake it off, and a portable vibrator to remove inches of it from any part of the body where it was unwanted. They also had a variety of internal ways of attacking it. They had purgatives and laxatives to rush the food through the system before it had a chance to add to the avoirdupois. They had materials to swell up in the stomach and leave little room for fattening foods. They had candy snacks to be taken before meals to forestall hunger at mealtime.

They had all kinds of drugs, some to stimulate metabolism, other to depress appetite, still others to dehydrate the body.

A favorite was one which miraculously slimmed the body down regardless of what or how much the individual ate. Hailed as an "amazing new drug," a TV commercial depicted a stout woman sitting at a table fading down to slimness, all the while eating like mad.

—JOSEPH J. SELDEN, from *The Golden Fleece*

1. The above passage begins with the words: "The ability to believe in magic," and continues to describe people who wanted so badly to lose weight that they were willing to try or do anything which claimed to be weight-losing.

Did you ever fool yourself? If so, tell about it. If not, tell about someone, real or imaginary, who did so.

2. Could it be that there is something rather mean about advertisers who make claims about their products which are only half-true?

For example: "You too can be the life of the party. Buy one of our banjos, learn to play it, and watch your popularity grow!"

You buy this banjo, but try as you will, the only result of your playing it is to drive people far away.

In one sentence or many, say what you think of advertisers who tell half-truths.

3. However, let's not drop the idea of half-truths. Sometimes the most honest people tell them. Write a page or so concerning a situation which, in your opinion, calls for the telling of a half-truth.

FASHIONS

THERE WERE HUGE HATS, tiny hats, hats with vast brims and microscopic crowns, hats which were not hats at all but wreaths about the hair; high fezzes perched atop the head; flat hats, dinner-plate size, which apparently had been thrown at the wearer from somewhere out in front and had been lashed where they landed with a sort of halter about the back of the head; straw birds' nests full of spring flowers, hats with a single long feather pointing anywhere—but why continue the interminable catalog of variations? It was characteristic of the times that a woman lunching at a New York tearoom in 1938 took the bread-basket off the table, inverted it on her head, and attracted no attention whatever.

—FREDERICK LEWIS ALLEN, from *Since Yesterday*

---

1. Sometime, during the past year or so, you must have seen someone wearing something which you considered rather outrageous. In a page or so, describe this strange sight.

2. Think of the absolute ecstasy felt by hat designers in the days recalled above!

Okay, be a hat designer. In a few paragraphs, describe the hat you designed for the exclusive use of the latest flame of the president of the local auto-racing association.

3. You have a secret yen to be different. In a page or so, tell of your efforts, successful or unsuccessful, to satisfy this secret yen.

FASHIONS

In his long passage down the road of time, man has painted, mutilated, and tattooed his body. He has adorned and covered it with leaves, shells, stones, feathers, skins, and almost every soft or flexible material found in nature. At a later period in his evolution he twisted grasses and spun fibers and filaments into a yarn. He then wove this yarn into a cloth which he used as a body covering.

—MILTON N. GROSS, from *History of Hosiery*

---

1. Tracing the history of any activity is a fascinating business. In a page or so, trace the personal history of your latest fashion fad. (Don't forget to say whether or not there are those who disapprove, and, if so, how you handle gripers of this sort.)

2. You are a proud parent, entering your three-year-old in a baby beauty contest. In a few paragraphs tell how you would decorate the three-year-old so that he or she will have the utmost opportunity of taking the blue ribbon.

154

Wʜᴀᴛ'ꜱ ʜᴀᴘᴘᴇɴɪɴɢ, I suspect, is that we're so afraid of being square that we're running around in circles, so worried that we might be "out" that we're trying frantically to be "in," right up there with the taste-makers, cavorting through the newest cultural craze and frenetically following the latest fashion and fad.

—ᴊᴜᴅɪᴛʜ ᴄʀɪꜱᴛ, from "When is it In and When is it Sick?"

1. Does your being "in" or "out" cause you much worry? If so, tell, in a few paragraphs, the substance of your worry. If not, tell your opinion of the worriers. If neither, give your definition of a "square."

2. Things come "in" and go "out" so fast! Today's craze may end tomorrow. Yet surely there must be "in" or "out" things which are permanent. In a few paragraphs, tell about some of these things which, in your life at least, you consider permanent.

3. In a page or so, describe a "tastemaker" you've known, the sort (according to Judith Crist in the passage above) "we're trying frantically to be right up there with."

DISCOVERY

MACHINES

"OH THE BRAIN, the brain!" exclaimed the pious Alderman, lifting up his hands. "Oh the nerves, the nerves; the mysteries of this machine called Man!"   —CHARLES DICKENS, from *Christmas Stories*

1. Consider the last seven words of the above passage: "the mysteries of this machine called Man."

In a page or so, reveal some of these mysteries.

2. The writers of science fiction have invented many robots. As a matter of fact, engineers and physicists have actually built many robots.

In a few paragraphs, say whether you think man will ever be able to build a robot superior to man.

3. You are a scientist with infinite skill and all the money necessary to purchase whatever material you need.

You decide to build the machine of your dreams. In a page or so, tell about its being built, and what you did with it when it was finished.

HOW DOES IT WORK?
What makes it tick?
How do they make . . .?

It used to be that the answers to these questions were self-evident. Loosen a few screws and the gas lamp would come apart in your hands—its separate parts and their principles of operation as obvious as a hammer. It used to be that a man could make, replace, or repair every machine, tool, or household item he owned. Often he had made it in the first place.

But today things aren't so simple. The watch you take apart is ruined for good. Inside a radio you find a mass of confused wires, tubes, and knobs as meaningless as a foreign language. And that is the problem exactly; science *is* a foreign language. The strange words (or worse, the familiar words used in strange ways) make science seem so different, so complicated, so impossible to understand that we are tempted to give up without even trying.   —RICHARD M. KOFF, from *How Does It Work?*

1. Are you a "tinkerer"? Is it next to impossible for you to leave things un-taken-apart? Surely it's a forgivable human frailty, to succumb to this temptation.

But when you can't put things together again, forgiveness doesn't come quite so easily.

In a page or so, describe a one-way tinkerer you've known.

2. You are a parent. You notice that your four-year-old boy is developing a tendency to take things apart and, in general, leave things in pretty much of a mess.

You don't want to frustrate the child by tying up his hands and feet, or locking him into an utterly empty room, but there are limits.

You have an idea. You will set him to work at something productive.

In a page or so, tell how you did this.

3. In a few paragraphs, describe the person who makes repairs at your house.

MACHINES

IF WE SURVIVE the leisure which the Atomic Age will bring, we may face a greater crisis. We still have the dreadful prospect of hour after hour, even day after day, with nothing significant to do. After we have read all the comic books, traveled all the miles, seen all the movies, listened to all the commercials, and drunk all the liquor we can stand, what shall we do then? Viscount Grey characterizes us as "pleasure-seeking but not pleasure-finding people."

—JAY B. NASH, from *The Philosophy of Recreation and Leisure*

---

1. One of the questions which a small child often throws at its mother is, "What should I do now?" Then the mother has to think of something to suggest to the child, to keep it from (shall we say it?) driving her nuts.

You are a mother (be a father, if you'd rather). You've had the above question thrown at you.

In a page or so, describe the asker of the question, the answer you gave, and your ideas for carrying out the suggestion.

162

2. Every one reaches the point of saturation, when he can absorb no more. You may love chocolate chip ice cream beyond all foods, but there is a limit to the amount you can eat. You may love to dance, but there is also a limit here.

Go back into your personal memory and dig out an experience of this sort. In a page or so, describe it.

3. Have you ever dreamed and dreamed of doing something, thought that if you could only have the chance of doing it you'd be the happiest person in the U.S.?

The opportunity arrived. You did it. Then what?

In a page or so, describe the dream, the doing, the "then what?"

MACHINES

W E NOW TAKE the automobile for granted, but there is still something arrogant about a driver propelling a contrivance fifteen times the human weight and ten times its size, past other human beings at a speed a dozen times their capacity to dodge it. It is a thousand times as arrogant when a thousand such contrivances whiz in and out of our main streets, forcing other chaps to take cover and taking the life of one human target every fourteen minutes. —CHARLES ABRAMS, from *The City Is the Frontier*

---

1. "Arrogant," as Abrams uses the word in the above passage, might mean "snooty," or "high-hat," or "high-and-mighty," or "over-proud", or even "holier-than-thou." Whatever he means exactly, he certainly conveys a picture.

In a page or so, convey your commentary upon the point of view expressed above.

2. In your opinion, who is really the boss: man, or the machines he has constructed? Write a page or so and put yourself in your narrative if you wish.

3. You are a super individualist, sworn never to use any sort of machine.

For a page or so, tell about your adventures during the course of a day's time. (Play fair, now. You can't just cop out. You've got to eat, go to work, keep yourself neat and clean, entertain yourself or others, and so on.)

Game for Anything

Science, it seems, is now well on the way,
    To achieve its considerate aims for us:
First machines to provide us with leisure to play,
    Then machines to play various games for us.
When machines do our work and machines do our play,
    We'll rejoice, for we'll then be in clover.
We'll have nothing to do all the livelong day—
    Till machines that do nothing take over!

—RICHARD ARMOUR

1. People used to walk and exercise their muscles. Now they ride in machines and don't exercise their muscles. If muscles don't get exercised they get flabby. Flabby muscles result in flabby people.

On the other hand, people can go a lot farther and a lot faster when they ride in machines.

In a page or so, tell some of the advantages and disadvantages you find in machines.

2. In a few paragraphs, tell about one of the machines or gadgets which has entered your life during your personal memory. Has it been good or bad for you?

3. Many people can hardly wait until they reach the age of retirement (they have a pension—their children have grown up and left home). Now they won't have to work. They'll have nothing to do but enjoy themselves.

Retirement time arrives. For a few weeks there is mad joy. Then, slowly, they begin to go crazy.

In one year you will have reached the time of retirement, as described above. In a page or so, tell your plans.

4. Referring to the fourth line of the above poem, tell, in a few paragraphs, about a machine you know that plays games for us. Invent a machine—at least on paper—if necessary.

164

"Look at it this way, Mom and Dad. If I had my own car, you'd be free. I could come and go as I had to, without bothering anybody or borrowing somebody else's car. The way it is now, if I use the family car, you're stuck until I get back. And if you use it when I need it, I'm stuck. That means I have to depend on my friends for a ride and trust my life to whatever driver wants to take me along, and you know how dangerous *that* could be. But you know I'm a careful driver, and I'd always be home on time, because I'd be in charge of the car. Besides that, I could run a lot of errands for the family and be *helpful* . . ."

—HENRY GREGOR FELSEN, from *A Teen-Ager's First Car*

1. Sometimes you've got to fight hard for the things you want. You've got to think up all sorts of dandy arguments to prove that your need is enormous.

In a page or so, tell about a situation in which you had to fight hard for the things you wanted, and recount some of the arguments you used. If not you, create someone.

2. You are a used-car salesman. The other day you showed a used car to a young man (or a young lady), who practically drooled over it, but said that his dad would have to come before he could say yes or no.

Now he's back at the used-car lot with his dad.

In a page or so, describe your customers and your experience with them.

3. It was a glorious Saturday morning in late April. You picked up your brand new second-hand car.

In a page or so, tell how you spent the day.

Medicine

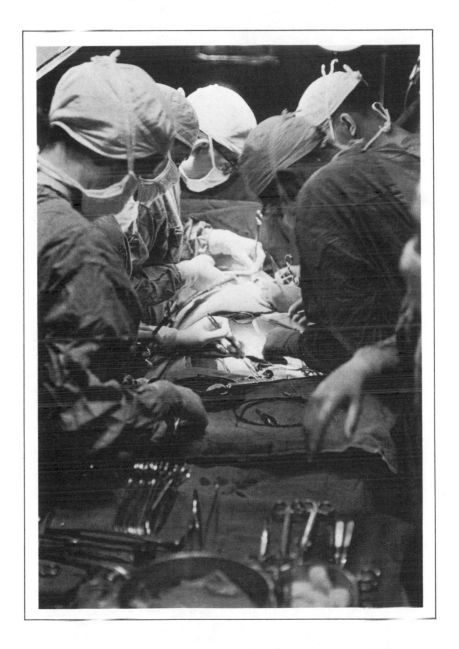

Suddenly he loved humanity as he loved the decent, clean rows of test tubes, and he prayed then the prayer of the scientist:

"God give me unclouded eyes and freedom from haste. God give me a quiet and relentless anger against all pretense and all pretentious work and all work left slack and unfinished. God give me a restlessness whereby I may neither sleep nor accept praise till my observed results equal my calculated results or in pious glee I discover and assault my error. God give me strength not to trust to God!"   —SINCLAIR LEWIS, from *Arrowsmith*

1. Each activity demands particular apparatus and particular abilities. In a page or so, tell what are the particular apparatus and the individual qualities for which you would pray, so that you might do work in which you would be happy, and of which you would be proud.

2. Consider the last sentence of the above passage. Notice that its last two words are "to God," and not "in God." In a few paragraphs, give your opinion concerning what Sinclair Lewis means to convey in this sentence.

3. In a page or so, tell how you, or someone you know, or a character of your imagination, "discovered and assaulted an error."

There was an infernal scream as the steel plunged into my skull. It sank more and more rapidly through the bone, and the pitch of its scream became louder and more piercing every second. I had just time to say to myself that it must be the electric trephine. They needn't have bothered to be so discreet about their whispering . . . ! My head throbbed and roared like a thousand-horsepower engine suddenly starting up. It thundered as if the infernal regions had opened or the earth were quaking. I never had a chance to think whether it was hurting me or not. Suddenly, there was a violent jerk, and the noise stopped. Having penetrated the skull the point was revolving freely in a space that offered no resistance. I felt a warm, silent rush of liquid inside my head, as if the blood were flowing *inward* from the hole which had been made.

—FRIGYES KARINTHY, from "Journey Round My Skull"

---

trephine: a rotary saw for removing a piece of bone from the skull

---

1. The above passage is from the story of a man who underwent a brain operation under local anesthetic. Though there was no pain, there were other sensations.

In a page or so, tell of an experience in which you suffered no pain, but during which there were plenty of other sensations.

2. Imagine the self-confidence it must take to do brain surgery. The slightest slip of the fingers, hesitation, misdirection, might make a permanent idiot of the patient, or paralyze him, or kill him.

In a page or so, tell of something you did, or should like to do, which calls for great self-confidence.

3. In a few paragraphs, outline a story concerning a person whose only hope of recovery is a dangerous operation.

■ MEDICINE ■

THERE ARE SELF-PROTECTIVE INSTINCTS in young children which impel them to seek foods needed at the moment by their body cells.

I made a study of children under ten years of age who lived on Vermont farms, in order that I might learn the workings of these instincts. I discovered that these young farm children chewed cornstalks, ate raw potatoes, raw carrots, raw peas, raw string beans, raw rhubarb, berries, green apples, ripe apples, the grapes that grow wild throughout the state, sorrel, timothy grass heads, and the part of the timothy stem that grows underground. They ate salt from the cattle box, drank water from the cattle trough, chewed hay, ate calf food and, by the handful, a dairy-ration supplement containing seaweed; they even filled their pockets with this, to eat during school.   —D. C. JARVIS, M.D., from *Folk Medicine*

---

1. It certainly is true, this "instinctive eating" by children of the correct and needed foods. But what about the opposite? Is there "instinctive non-eating" by children of the incorrect and unnecessary foods?

Not on your life!

In a page or so, tell of any melancholy experience you may have had from eating unwisely and unfortunately.

2. What about actions that you instinctively feel that you should do?

Write a page-or-more-long fantasy. You are in class, engaged in some activity or other directed by your teacher. Suddenly you are overtaken with the instinctive certainty that you should be doing something else (something which does not require you to leave the room).

What is this instinctive something? How do you handle the situation?

3. How about your dog, or other pet? In a paragraph or so, tell how you have, in training it, squashed a few of its instincts.

MEDICINE

At about eight o'clock on Monday morning, September 25, 1944, a ragged, aimless old man of eighty-two collapsed on the sidewalk on Dey Street, near the Hudson Terminal. Innumerable people must have noticed him, but he lay there alone for several minutes, dazed, doubled up with abdominal cramps, and in an agony of retching. Then a policeman came along. Until the policeman bent over the old man, he may have supposed that he had just a sick drunk on his hands; wanderers dropped by drink are common in that part of town in the early morning. It was not an opinion that he could have held for long. The old man's nose, lips, ears, and fingers were sky-blue. The policeman went to a telephone and put in an ambulance call to Beekman-Downtown Hospital, half a dozen blocks away. The old man was carried into the emergency room there at eight-thirty. By that time, he was unconscious and the blueness had spread over a large part of his body.   —BERTON ROUECHÉ, from *Eleven Blue Men*

---

1. One of the first things you learn when you study first aid is that you must never jump to conclusions about the nature of someone's distress. In other words, if you see someone lying on the sidewalk, don't just assume that he's drunk, and pass by him with a sneer.

In a few paragraphs, tell about an accident case you've seen, or read about.

2. You have been stricken by a sudden attack of something or other. Though your mind is working away energetically, you are temporarily speechless, and your body is temporarily paralyzed.

In a page or so, tell what runs through your mind while you are waiting to be helped.

3. In a few paragraphs, tell why or why not you would like to work on the crew of an ambulance.

MEDICINE

AN EXPERT HYPNOTIST can persuade a subject not to see a certain person, and such is the power of the mind that the subject may be unable to do so even if that person is standing in full view. The subject will go to extraordinary lengths to "explain away" the invisible man even when the latter tries to prove that he is present: The individual under hypnosis may eventually get hysterical if, for example, he sees what he believes are unattached articles of furniture moving around the room.

—ARTHUR C. CLARKE, from *Profiles of the Future*

---

1. You have been granted the ability to make one person, and only one, disappear. In a few paragraphs, describe that person and tell why you chose him or her.

2. It is said that a super spy would find the use of hypnosis extremely valuable. For one or more pages you are a super spy with the ability to hypnotize whomever you wish, whenever you wish. In a page or so, tell one of your most thrilling experiences.

3. Reread with great care the last sentence of the above passage.
Now, be fiendish!
You have the ability called for in the sentence you have just carefully reread. Someone you don't care for a bit is visiting at your house. Although you'd like very much to get rid of this person, your natural politeness forbids you to up and say, "Get out!"
What would you do?

space fiction

"Every one of them died of the same thing. There were no external marks, and no indication of injury. Ultimately, each of them died of shock. Or fear. Or both."

The doctor cleared his throat. "I believe we're dealing solely with a matter of adjustment. Apparently these men have been faced with something that they've never met before. Something completely foreign to their experience, and something with which their nervous systems cannot cope. They've run into something so startling, or frightening, or stupendous, that their minds saw no escape but total and immediate breakdown. It was adjust or collapse, and being unable to adjust, they collapsed, and the shock was too much for their systems. So they died. Of fear, if you will— there's nothing else to blame."

The director toyed with his pipe. "And your recommendations, Dr. Marks? Shall we just keep feeding good men to this thing?"

"Not quite. As I said, it's a problem in adjustment. We need a man with a high adjustment threshold—a *very* high threshold. We need a man with a cast-iron nervous system, a nervous system that can adjust to *anything,* regardless of impact or excitation of any sort. Give us that man, and I'd agree to another stab at it."

The director knocked out his pipe and placed it in his pocket with finality. "Well, Mac?" he said gently.

McEvoy smiled. "Down in the recording vault," he said quietly, "we have a cross-index file. I think I'll spend a sleepless night or two down there."   —ALAN E. NOURSE, from "High Threshold"

---

1. And so the hunt begins for a person with super nerves. Suppose you were writing a science fiction story, in which a super-someone was needed. In a page or so, tell the type of super quality which was needed, and describe the type of person you would find to fit this need.

2. Surely, at some time or other, you, or someone of your acquaintance, have been confronted by a mysterious, frightening, dangerous situation. In a page or so, tell about it.

3. In a few paragraphs, describe the person you know (this person might well be yourself) who seems best fitted to progress smoothly over the rocky, rutted road of living.

Destruction of a node sent a restless shiver through the unigen. A node represented an integral fraction of the unigen's brain; it had been conditioned to modify a definite class of thoughts. When the node was destroyed, the thinking in the class was curtailed until another node could be produced and endowed with the same precise channels.

The implications of the event were further cause for anxiety. The metal energy-eaters on another planet used the same technique—a stream of electrons smashing across the center of the node, to upset the equilibrium. The flash was a flash of released energy, which the metal ovoids were able to absorb. Apparently the land-worm had been surprised by the explosion and destroyed—possibly mistaking the nodes for some less energetic type of creature.   —JACK VANCE, from "Winner Lose All"

---

1. How many times have you read the above passage? If you understand it, congratulations. If you don't, don't worry.

Science fiction writers manufacture ideas in droves. What a world we'd have, populated by their creatures!

Have you ever "manufactured" a creature? If so, tell about it in a page or so. If not, manufacture one now, or tell about one you've come across.

2. You are a unigen, as presented in the above passage. In a page or so, tell about your family.

3. Your dearest friend needs your help badly, has called upon you to help dispel the jitters left from an awful nightmare. You decide that the best thing to do is to go somewhere, which will soothe an overexcited mind.

In a few paragraphs, say where you took your friend, and why you chose that particular place.

"I . . . BROKE THE QUARANTINE ON PHARONA," said Sally. "It . . . it was terrible, Ben! They're . . . dying there by . . . by millions. Women. Only women. And girls. And nobody knows why. Their bodies give off cosmic rays, and they die. That's all. There's no real night on Pharona, you know, only twilight, so it was only the day before I left that they . . .

discovered that women who have the plague glow, too. They get . . . phosphorescent. They don't feel badly, only oppressed. They get fever, and cosmic rays come from them, and in the dark they shine faintly, and they get weaker and weaker, and then they die. And men are immune, and they are going crazy! Their wives and sweethearts and daughters and mothers dying before their eyes. And they're not even in danger—"

"Don't tell me now if you don't want to," said Ben.

"I . . . think I'm all right. I must be!" said Sally. "I was twelve days on the way. If . . . if I'd had the plague I'd have died, wouldn't I? At least I'd be sick by now! But I'm not. Only . . . I couldn't sleep much, Ben."   —MURRAY LEINSTER, from "Plague"

---

1. Did you ever think of all the terrible germs to which you have been exposed, and the few that have taken hold of you? Of those that have, or, at least of the illnesses which they have caused you, tell, in a page or so, about the most miserable.

2. You are coming down with a terrible and very contagious illness. At least you think you are.

You have been invited to a party at which "the one" will be present. It is possible, because of the imminence of this terrible and very dangerous illness with which you think you are coming down, that this party will be your last opportunity to see "the one."

In a page or so, describe your feelings and your actions.

3. You are a "worry-wart" parent, sure that entire battalions of deadly creatures, in size from invisible to gigantic, are everlastingly lying in wait for your child.

Describe your relationship with your child. A few paragraphs should contain your thoughts.

SPACE FICTION

BEFORE WILLIAMS WENT into the future he bought a camera and a tape recording machine and learned shorthand. That night, when all was ready, we made coffee and put out brandy and glasses against his return.

"Good-bye," I said. "Don't stay too long."

"I won't," he answered.

I watched him carefully, and he hardly flickered. He must have made a perfect landing on the very second he had taken off from. He seemed not a day older; we had expected he might spend several years away.

"Well?"

"Well," said he, "let's have some coffee."

I poured it out, hardly able to contain my impatience. As I gave it to him I said again, "Well?"

"Well, the thing is, I can't remember."

"Can't remember? Not a thing?"

He thought for a moment and answered sadly, "Not a thing."

"But your notes? The camera? The recording machine?"

The notebook was empty, the indicator of the camera rested at "1" where we had set it, the tape was not even loaded into the recording machine.

"But good heavens," I protested, "why? How did it happen? Can you remember nothing at all?"

"I can remember only one thing."

"What was that?"

"I was shown everything, and I was given the choice whether I should remember it or not after I got back."

"And you chose not to? But what an extraordinary thing to—"

"Isn't it?" he said. "One can't help wondering why."

—W. HILTON-YOUNG, "The Choice"

---

1. This little science fiction tale is a satire, a sort of laugh at the "time machine" stories. Read it carefully, to get it straight. Then, in a page or so, write a "review" of it: a criticism, giving any ideas you may have concerning its author, or Williams, its time-traveling hero.

2. It would seem that the relationship of time and men has always been a source of puzzlement. In a page or so, tell the greatest puzzlement with time that you can remember.

3. Suppose you were, by some strange happening, granted the privilege of one, and only one, voyage *backward* in time. In a few paragraphs, say where you would choose to go.

4. Think again about the decision Williams was asked to make in the tale: "I was given the choice whether I should remember it or not after I got back." In a few paragraphs, give some reasons Williams might have used in choosing to remember nothing.

SPACE FACT

A MYSTERIOUS EXPLOSION at 10:11 p.m. EST, April 13, apparently ripped open an oxygen tank in the service compartment of the Apollo 13 spacecraft. The three-man crew was four fifths of the way to the moon.

As a result of the rupture, gas—which was supposed to feed into fuel cells to produce electricity vital to the ship's functions—escaped uselessly into space. For a time, it was feared that the violently bucking spacecraft would hurtle uncontrolled into deep space, consigning the crewmen to death. Even after the ship had been stabilized, the threat remained that there would not be enough oxygen for the men to breathe.

—U.S. *News & World Report* of April 27, 1970

1. What faith they have, these astronauts! Their lives depend upon the skill of the engineers who design their spacecraft, and upon the care and craftsmanship of each workman who helps in its construction.

In a page or so, tell of a situation in which your life and/or safety has depended upon someone else's skill and care.

2. Of course, if it weren't for our certainty that the "laws of nature" would never be broken, we would never dare to send out spacecraft. (Suppose, for instance, the laws of gravity started flipflopping around!)

Write, upon a page or so, an imaginary episode in which a law of nature was somehow broken.

3. You are a child again, planning your first small voyage of exploration.

In a few paragraphs, tell where you intend to go, and what you hope to accomplish.

IN COMPARING THE EARTH with its neighbors within the planetary system, it is safe to say, without running the risk of seeming parochial, that our planet is unique. In fact, it is the only one with a world-wide ocean. All the others, along with their moons, including our own satellite, are covered either by absolutely dry desert or by vast layers of ice and frozen methane and ammonia. Were it not for a peculiarity in the earth's evolution, its entire surface would consist of water extending from pole to pole, without a speck of land. If the earth were a smooth sphere, the quantity of water in the oceans would be sufficient to envelop the entire globe with a depth of 7,500 feet, in which case this planet would have a truly liquid surface. —HEINZ HABER, from *Our Blue Planet*

---

1. Are you proud of the fact that Earth is the only heavenly body (planet, moon, or other) of our solar system which has a worldwide ocean? If you are proud of that fact, say why, in a few paragraphs. If you are not proud of that fact, say why not, in a few paragraphs.

2. Suppose you had a sore throat and the doctor said to you, "Open wide, I want to get a good look, and then paint it with antiseptic."
You opened wide. You really tried hard, because you wanted to be as cooperative as possible.
After he'd finished he said to you, "My, but you have a fine throat for looking and painting."
In a few paragraphs, say how you felt because he said this.

3. Reread the last sentence of the above passage. Then imagine it is many, many years from now, and the mountains have all but worn away, and the earth is just about to become a smooth sphere.
You are attending a conference of scientists who are trying to decide what to do about the coming disaster. In a page or so, describe that conference.

◾◾◾◾◾◾◾◾ SPACE FACT ◾◾◾◾◾◾◾◾

THE ASTRONAUTS ARE SCHEDULED to land on the moon at 45 centi-lunours past 22 lunours in the ninth lune of the 585th lunation, according to Dr. Kenneth L. Franklin, astronomer at the Hayden Planetarium.
To earthlings, that's 9:55 P.M., Eastern standard time on April 15, 1970. For the astronauts landing at Fra Mauro, it will be "early morning," with the sun 11 degrees above the lunar horizon.
—from *The New York Times*

---

1. You can bring your earthly food with you to a strange heavenly body, and your earthly paraphernalia, but you can't bring your earthly time, because time is a strictly local affair.

Other things besides time on heavenly bodies are also local affairs, and must be adapted to.

In a page or so, tell about your having to adapt to a strictly local affair. If not you, tell about a character of your imagination.

2. There is an old song that begins: "I wish I had all the money that I've spent on women." How about minutes? Do you sometimes wish you had all the minutes that you've spent on—well, on what? In a page or so, tell about the time when you wasted a lot of minutes.

3. Let's say that you can rearrange your day, and spend the twenty-four hours in any combination of ways you think best. Give the schedule you'd choose.

SPACE FACT

At every moment of our lives we are somewhere in space and somewhere in time. The ratio between a change of our position in space and the time that it takes it to happen is our speed. That sounds perfectly simple and straightforward. But suppose you are on a jet plane from New York to San Francisco and someone asks you what time it is. You may answer, "Well, by my watch it's eleven o'clock, but that's New York time. We left New York at nine and we're due in San Francisco at 11:55 their time, three hours earlier than New York time, so we're due there in three hours and fifty-five minutes and we've been in the air two hours. If we're two-sixths or one-third of the way, we're probably in the Central Time belt which is one hour earlier than New York time. In answer to your question, sir, it's ten o'clock."

—ELIZABETH A. WOOD, from *Science for the Airplane Passenger*

---

1. One of the odd things about time is that it seldom seems the same twice in succession; for instance, watching a good TV show for half an hour, and waiting for someone for half an hour.

Tell of several experiences you have had when time seemed inordinately long or short.

2. Thoreau said, "Time is but the stream I go a-fishing in." In a paragraph, say what you think he meant by this remark.

3. What is time, anyway? Write at least one page.

4. You are a parent. You have just told your ten-year-old child that each time a person goes westward around the world, he gains a day.

Your ten-year-old child nods, thinks for a moment, then asks: "Well, if I kept on going around the world, would I ever grow old?"

That night, after your child has been sent to bed, you begin to think about the question. You sit down and write a few paragraphs answering his question.

What was the explanation you gave?

■■■■■■■■■■■ SPACE FACT ■■■■■■■■■■■

THE KIDS HAVE ALREADY "blasted off"; they can buy space suits and one-kid rockets at almost any toy store. The heroes of the comics are fighting bad men on Mars. The subtler heroes of science fiction have pushed their operations beyond the Milky Way. Space has become the wild frontier of the modern imagination. To those who find the earth too well known, too tame, too dull, it offers unbounded adventure.

—JONATHAN NORTON LEONARD, from *Flight Into Space*

---

1. Observe the last sentence of the above passage. It suggests that when the world becomes too boring, you can blast off, seek another home, far away, far away.

In a page or so, say why, or why not, you would rather be on earth than any other place in space.

2. The author of the above passage claims that space "has become the wild frontier of the modern imagination." If you agree with this, say why in a few paragraphs. If you feel that something other than space is the "wild frontier," describe it.

exploration

Suddenly i found myself at the bottom of a black pit, clawing at the sides, attempting to escape. Leering into the pit was Satan, an evil-looking creature with the head of a demon and the body of a spider. He was sneering at me and uttering the words "Alone! Alone! Alone!" The words echoed throughout the pit like a curse, an affliction from which I could not escape.

As I tried in vain to climb the walls of the pit, I noticed that it was completely devoid of color. The bottom and sides were black and slimy, the smell was foul and rotten. There was no one with whom to share my plight; I was alone in the pit.

—STANLEY KRIPPNER, from "Of Hell and Heavenly Blue"

1. The above passage tells of a voyage of discovery, all inside a human brain which had been stimulated by the drug LSD.

Strange, this mind of ours, which can "see" so many things that never existed. In a page or so, tell of a time when you imagined, sleeping or waking, some terrifying sight.

2. The last sentence of the above passage speaks of "no one with whom to share my plight."

Look around you. Do you see anyone with whom you'd most like to "share your plight"? If so, describe this person, and say why. If not, tell of someone else, real or imaginary.

3. In a few paragraphs, give any ideas you may have concerning the problems of taking drugs and drug addiction.

This was to be our final session in The Valley. Six full seasons we had excavated there, and season after season had drawn a blank; we had worked for months at a stretch and found nothing, and only an excavator knows how desperately depressing that can be; we had almost made up our minds that we were beaten, and were preparing to leave The Valley and try our luck elsewhere; and then—hardly had we set hoe to ground in our last despairing effort than we made a discovery that far exceeded our wildest dreams. Surely, never before in the whole history of excavation has a full digging season been compressed within the space of five days.

Let me try and tell the story of it all. It will not be easy, for the dramatic suddenness of the initial discovery left me in a dazed condition, and the months that have followed have been so crowded with incident that I have hardly had time to think. Setting it down on paper will perhaps give me a chance to realize what has happened and all that it means.

—HOWARD CARTER and A. C. MACE, from "The Tomb of Tutankhamen"

1. The world of the past seems to have endless fascination, at least for some people.

If the world of the past fascinates you, tell, in a few paragraphs, why. If the world of the past does not fascinate you, tell, in a few paragraphs, why not.

2. The authors of the above passage say that they had searched, season after season, and had found nothing. They had almost made up their minds that they were beaten, and were ready to give up. And then . . . !

In a page or so, recall a search you know of, seemingly hopeless, which ended in success.

3. There are those who have proved to be more important to a community after they left it than when they inhabited it. In a page or so, tell of someone of this type.

EXPLORATION

THE ASTONISHMENT which I felt on first seeing a party of Fuegians on a wild and broken shore will never be forgotten by me, for the reflection at once rushed into my mind—such were our ancestors. These men were absolutely naked and bedaubed with paint, their long hair was tangled, their mouths frothed with excitement, and their expression was wild, startled, and distrustful. They possessed hardly any arts, and like wild animals lived on what they could catch; they had no government, and were merciless to every one not of their own small tribe. He who has seen a savage in his native land will not feel much shame, if forced to acknowledge that the blood of some more humble creature flows in his veins. For my own part I would as soon be descended from that heroic little monkey, who braved his dreaded enemy in order to save the life of his keeper; or from that old baboon, who, descending from the mountains, carried away in triumph his young comrade from a crowd of astonished dogs—as from a savage who delights to torture his enemies, offers up bloody sacrifices, practices infanticide without remorse, treats his wives like slaves, knows no decency, and is haunted by the grossest superstitions.

—CHARLES DARWIN, from "The Descent of Man"

1. Charles Darwin, author of the above passage, saw the Fuegians —wild inhabitants of Tierra del Fuego in the extreme south of South America—in 1832, when he was twenty-three years old. Many years later, when he had reached the conclusion that man had not been specially created, but had ascended from a long, long past, he remembered those wild Fuegians, and that he had thought, at the time he saw them, "such were our ancestors."

Play a sort of game. Think of five people you know, each of whom might be said to have inherited the major part of his nature from a different animal.

In five or so paragraphs, describe each person.

2. It is not only the Fuegians who are "bedaubed with paint, their long hair . . . tangled."

In a page or so, describe such a one whom you have seen yourself, and say why you think this person has so departed from the more usual way of appearing before his fellow man.

3. In a page or so, tell about "that heroic little monkey" (mentioned in the above passage), and/or "that old baboon."

EXPLORATION

SHOPPING IN A SUPERMARKET in the postwar years was like walking into an Oriental bazaar. The housewife clutched her shopping list as though she were trying to hold onto her senses as she wheeled a shopping cart down the canyons of multicolored, multisized, and multibranded goods. Everything was "one grand shout," as one researcher described its impact on the housewife. "Her pulse rate and respiration changed. She was poised like a cat, ready to spring when she saw something new and better. Quicker. Tastier. Newer. A better buy. A handier spout. A more promising promise," was the way *The Wedge,* an agency house organ, described it. And since she spent on an average 20 minutes for her tour of shopping, some agency mathematician figured out that some 300 to 400 items a minute clawed for her attention.

—JOSEPH J. SELDEN, from *The Golden Fleece*

1. Think back. It is many years ago. You are quite young. It is the week before your birthday. For the first time in your life you are going to be taken to a toy store. How do you feel? What are you thinking?

2. In supermarkets you have often seen mothers pushing little children around in shopping carts. They push them, primarily, because little children can be nuisances.

Perhaps you approve of kids riding in shopping carts, perhaps not.

However you think on this subject, write a few hundred words presenting your ideas as to what should be done with little children when mothers must take them along wherever they go.

3. In the above-quoted passage, there is a description of a housewife in a supermarket: "Her pulse rate and respiration changed." This was her *physiological* response to her emotional condition.

Tell of a time when you responded physiologically to an emotional experience such as fear or guilt. If such a thing never happened to you, tell of it happening to someone else, real or imaginary.

EXPLORATION

JUST AS THERE ARE MANY who can't see the reasons for blazing trails to outer space, there are also those who see no reason on earth for plunging beneath the sea as men are beginning to do. If God had wanted us to fly, we'd have wings, say these skeptics. And if we were intended to dwell in the sea, we'd have fins and gills.

—D. S. HALACY, JR., from *Beyond Tomorrow*

1. There's always somebody to say, "What's the use of doing that? You're just wasting your time."

And yet, on the other hand, some things certainly do seem foolhardy and dangerous.

You are a parent. One evening, just after you've finished supper, your sixteen-year-old daughter informs you that in ten minutes Freddie McChopper will drop down onto the front lawn to take her for a ride in his new helicopter.

In a few pages, tell the story of the next fifteen minutes in the lives of you, your sixteen-year-old daughter, and young Freddie McChopper.

2. In a page or so, tell about some of the things you'd like to have somebody invent during the next fifteen years.

3. In a few paragraphs, tell about some of the things which nearly everybody else thinks are wonderful, but which you yourself think are terrible.

4. If you could be any animal you wished (this includes all members of the animal kingdom, from amoeba to man, including the birds and the bees), say which one you'd choose to be, and explain why you'd choose to be that one.

EXPLORATION

No FURTHER OBSERVATIONS on these "little animals" appear to have been reported until more than a year later. But in a letter written in December, 1675, van Leeuwenhoek again alludes to them briefly, in the following words:

> In the past summer I have made many observations upon various waters, and in almost all discovered an abundance of very little and odd animalcules, whereof some were incredibly small, less even than the animalcules which others have discovered in water, and which have been called by the name of Water-flea, or Water-louse.

ANTON VAN LEEUWENHOEK, from a letter, 1675

---

1. Anton van Leeuwenhoek lived in Holland, was a successful business man who, in his spare time, engaged in his hobby of grinding lenses. He examined, under these lenses, almost everything possible. He saw tiny

creatures in water, moving with great energy and spirit. He kept notes about what he saw, he told people, he wrote letters. And he has everlasting fame.

Do you have a hobby? If so, write a page or so telling about it and explaining why or why not you expect it to bring you everlasting fame. If you do not have a hobby, make one up.

2. Most things that we know were discovered by someone, sometime. But some things we know were never "discovered." We don't "learn" these things. We just know them. This knowledge is "instinctive" knowledge.

In a few paragraphs, give some examples of instinctive knowledge.

3. In a page or so, tell about the time you came upon something completely new to you, and the joy, the horror, or the amazement you felt.

COMMUNICATION

ADVERTISING

Consider the detergent whose commercial you hate the most. You may, if you wish, question whether it actually does make clothes whiter than white; you may doubt that it gets out more stubborn dirt than other washday products leave in; you may wonder whether it really leaves your clothes squeaky-clean and ever so manageable. But there is one thing you may bank on with a considerable degree of confidence. It *is* a detergent.

Doubt, if you wish, that Winston tastes good—but doubt not that Winston is a cigarette! —DAVID G. LYON, from *Off Madison Avenue*

1. Do just what is suggested in the first sentence of the above passage. Then, in a page or so, describe the commercial and say why you hate it.

2. The above passage is tricky. The author says, in defense of the commercial, "Well, maybe it makes you sick, but you've got to admit that it tells you about something that really exists!" How'd you like it if it tried to make you believe in something that didn't exist!

In a few paragraphs, be just as tricky: say, for instance, why something is good just because it isn't bad.

3. In a page or so, tell about the time that you, or someone you know, were the victim of a "snow job."

Jim Dumps was a most unfriendly man
Who lived his life on the hermit plan.
　He'd never stop for a friendly smile
　But trudged along in his moody style.
Till "Force" one day was served to him.
Since then they call him Sunny Jim.
　　　—MARTIN MAYER,
　　from *Madison Avenue, U.S.A.*

1. The above verse was part of an advertising campaign to promote the sale of the ready-to-serve cereal, "Force."

Isn't it a wonderful thing, that the act of buying and using a particular advertised product can make such a difference in your life, that these substances can help you!

Fewer dates than a ———. Stomach sour as a ———. Breath bad as a ———. Dopey as a ———. Stupid as a ———. Less energy than a ———.

You are the aide to a writer of advertisements, called in to help out. The help needed is to fill in the above dashes.

Do so.

2. Amazing, too, how quickly you can change following the purchase and application of an advertised product!

In a page or so, tell about someone who suddenly changed enormously.

3. In a page or so, tell about the most unfriendly person you have ever known.

ADVERTISING

THIRD, the critics are particularly anguished by the *modus operandi* of advertising which selects, from the enormous range of human impulses of which man is capable, primarily the discreditable ones, because they have been found to be the most profitable. Fear, jealousy, envy, ambition, snobbery, greed, lust, and other appeals antithetical to society, are incessantly played up in popular ads to the disfigurement of human values. Such concepts as love, manliness, femininity, friendship are portrayed as though the very real human values they represent are attainable through the purchase of a new shaving lotion, a new deodorant, a new car. Man is conditioned by the ads to regulate his conduct in large measure by external considerations.   —JOSEPH J. SELDEN, from *The Golden Fleece*

---

1. The above passage does not paint a pretty picture of the advertising business, or of human nature for that matter.

Did you ever know anyone who bought a certain kind of car, not because he needed one, but because he wanted people to think he was rich and sporty? Did you ever know anyone who bought a certain kind of perfume because she wanted to be ultra-attractive? Did you ever know anyone who started smoking cigarettes because he wanted to be "in" with a certain group?

Do you think it's necessary to buy things and do things, not because you want to, but because other people (you hope) will think you want to?

Write a page or so discussing the above question.

2. Mary (John) Jones is an "in" sort of person. Write a page or so describing Mary (John) Jones.

ADVERTISING

A NEW MOTOR CARRIAGE which, if the preliminary tests prove successful is expected will revolutionize the mode of travel on highways and do away with the horse as a means of transportation, is being made in this city. It is quite probable that within a short time one may be able to see an ordinary carriage in almost every respect running along the streets or climbing country hills without visible means of propulsion. This carriage is being built by J. F. Duryea, the designer, and E. F. Markham, who have been at work on it for over a year. The vehicle was designed by C. E. Duryea, a bicycle manufacturer of Peoria, Ill., and he communicated the scheme to his brother.   —Advertisement in *Springfield Evening Union*, 1893

---

1. Everything had a beginning. Each thing was new once. There was a time when the automobile was new, when as yet very few people had heard of it. They had to be persuaded that it was here to stay!

(Now we can't even get rid of the wrecked ones!)

The above passage comes from an advertisement in an 1893 newspaper. Nearly eighty years ago!

Push yourself ahead two and a half generations. It is the year 2052. You are looking at an advertisement from a 1973 newspaper.

In a few paragraphs, write that advertisement.

2. There seems to be a tendency in men and women to cling to their past, to think of their early days as the best days. Maybe it hasn't happened to you yet, but there is little doubt that it will.

As you did in the first question, push yourself ahead. Not so far this time—make it one and a half generations. You are deep in animated discussion with your sixteen-year-old grandchild, defending your "good old days" against your grandchild's insistence that the good old days were awful.

In a page or so, reproduce that discussion.

3. You have been granted the money, and all else necessary, to start the manufacture of anything you want. In a page or so, describe the article you will manufacture, and tell your plans for introducing it to the public.

ADVERTISING

THE AVERAGE CONSUMER, poor dear, is now subjected to 10,000 commercials a year. Make sure that she knows the name of the product being advertised in your commercial. Repeat it, *ad nauseam,* throughout. Show it in at least one title. And show her the package which you want her to recognize in the store.

Make your product the hero of the commercial, as it is the hero of our famous commercial for Maxwell House Coffee—just a coffeepot and a cup of coffee—"good to the last drop." (I did not invent this slogan; Theodore Roosevelt did.)

—DAVID OGILVY, from *Confessions of an Advertising Man*

---

1. Oh, the ear-battering of it! And yet in spite of the fact that they know how cruel they are, how unhappy they make people, manufacturers keep right on polluting the air waves with stories of how great they are.

You are a manufacturer. There was a time when you polluted the air waves with the best of them. But something has happened to you. You've grown soft, and your conscience aches when you think of the pain you've brought to so many.

You give a speech to the National Manufacturers Association, telling about your change of heart, and pleading with them to do the same.

In a page or so, write that speech.

2. In the second paragraph of the above passage, Mr. Ogilvy says "Make your product the hero." What could Mr. Ogilvy possibly mean by this? How could a *product* be a *hero?*

In a few paragraphs, outline a story in which a product is a hero.

3. Pick someone to be the villain of the next story you write, and say, in a few paragraphs, why you picked this creature.

TELEVISION

A WOMAN WHO COMPLAINED at a PTA meeting that her children watched too much TV admitted that she'd never really tried to restrict them. She sighed, "The only peace I get is when the kids are glued to the idiot box. It may not be good for them, but it keeps them quiet."

She was asked, "Do you restrict the kind of programs they may watch?"

"No." Defeatedly, "The worse the program is for them, the quieter it seems to keep them. Otherwise they're under my feet."

—SAMM SINCLAIR BAKER, from *The Permissible Lie*

1. Here's an odd thing. The woman in the passage above speaks of her TV set as "the idiot box." She also says that very likely TV may not be good for her children. And yet she seems to be glad for them to watch it because it "keeps them quiet."

Perhaps she feels that it's worse for her children to be noisy than to watch the idiot box which is probably not good for them.

Do you understand exactly what she is trying to say? If you do, explain it in a few paragraphs. If you don't, tell how you feel about TV.

2. What does the woman mean by saying that the worse the program is for her children, the quieter it seems to keep them?

3. What is your dream type of TV program? Pretend you've just written one. Tell about it, and choose TV actors and/or singers to be in the show.

If you didn't write a show, write a commercial.

TELEVISION

IN A BOSTON SUBURB, a nine-year-old boy reluctantly showed his father a report card heavily decorated with red marks, then proposed one way of getting at the heart of the matter: they could give the teacher a box of poisoned chocolates for Christmas. "It's easy, Dad, they did it on television last week. A man wanted to kill his wife, so he gave her candy with poison in it and she didn't know who did it."

In Brooklyn, New York, a six-year-old son of a policeman asked his father for real bullets because his little sister "doesn't die for real when I shoot her like they do when Hopalong Cassidy kills 'em."

In Los Angeles, a housemaid caught a seven-year-old boy in the act of sprinkling ground glass into the family's lamb stew. There was no malice behind the act. It was purely experimental, having been inspired by curiosity to learn whether it would really work as well as it did on television.

—NORMAN COUSINS, from *The Saturday Review*

1. There's been much talk concerning the terrible effect of television horror tales upon young and impressionable minds.

And, contrariwise, there's been much talk claiming that the effects are not harmful.

In a page or so, discuss the matter from your own point of view, citing any and all evidence that you can bring to bear.

2. Surely, at some time, you have been an influence for good or ill upon someone. In a few paragraphs, tell about it.

TELEVISION

Oɴᴇ ᴄʜɪʟᴅ ᴡʀᴏᴛᴇ to TV entertainer Shari Lewis: "Your show is stupid and I always hate it every week, but I have to watch it because my sister watches it and we only have one television set. I hate to watch nothing worse than your stupid show so try to make it a better show this week. Your friend, Everett." —SAMM SINCLAIR BAKER, from *The Permissible Lie*

1. Everett's in a bad way, poor fellow. He's on what's known as the "horns of a dilemma." One horn: he's watching a TV show he hates. This makes him extremely unhappy. The other horn: he's not watching any TV show at all. This also makes him extremely unhappy.

What will he do?

Here's another example of someone on the horns of a dilemma:

Private John Jones is a soldier on the battlefield. He's scared witless of getting shot. There are two things he can do. He can stay on the battlefield,

204

or he can leave the battlefield. If he leaves the battlefield, one of his officers will shoot him for desertion. If he stays on the battlefield, the enemy will shoot him.

Have you ever been on the horns of a dilemma? Write about that dilemma. If you've never been on the horns of a dilemma, write about someone else being there (someone real or imaginary).

2. There is something else Everett could do to amuse himself. He could read a good book.

How do you feel about this? Write a few paragraphs on the following subject: "I would (would not) rather read a good book than watch a television program."

3. How about that sister (it could just as well be a brother) who dictates the program which will be watched? Do you, or do any of your friends have this sort of problem? Set down your ideas for its solution.

TELEVISION

My own school days were pre-TV, yet I recall next to nothing of physiology. Being a somewhat squeamish child, I usually turned my eyes away whenever an anatomy chart was unrolled. What I looked like inside never excited my curiosity, and until television came along and forced the facts on me, I kept confusing the human body with a drawing of Watt's steam engine. There, I've said it: for me, television succeeded where the school system failed. So if the Department of Education will kindly step aside, I'll demonstrate how simple the study of the human body can be, thanks to TV:

The Head: The top of the head (which science used to think housed a brain) actually is divided into three cells, or chambers. Two are filled with electrical charges which spark a lot, while the third contains a suspension coil spring from a 1954 Buick. (There are some heads in which this last chamber accommodates, instead of the spring, a small backsmith shop complete with hammer and anvil, but such cases, happily, seem rare). The chambers, from left to right, are for (1) Tension, (2) Pain, and (3) Jittery Nerves, and all are capable of lighting up brightly depending on what you've been up to. For a really first-class headache, it is important that all three chambers be in good working order.

The middle head takes in the nose and front of the face as far back as the ears. This is the S zone, "S" being the scientific symbol for Sinus. The S zone is pretty much like an ordinary kitchen sink faucet (without washers, of course) and is composed chiefly of membranes in need of shrinking.

Directly behind the S zone is the Cough Control Nerve Center. People with weak cough control nerves are apt to be bores at the theater.

Oh, yes, I almost forgot. The middle head also houses the teeth, whose function is the collection of tiny food particles which, in turn, decay the teeth. Thus, Mother Nature takes care of her own.

—W. F. MIKSCH, from "Inside Everybody, with TV"

---

1. What the writer is saying here is an excellent description of what actually occurs on TV screens. There is the use of imagery to put across a fact.

If someone says to you "Her teeth are like stars, they come out at night," you laugh, but you immediately know that she has false teeth.

Suppose you had to transfer that bit of imagery from words to pictures. How would you do it?

In at least a paragraph for each, present several facts, using imagery (as above), and then tell how you would transfer the words to pictures.

2. There is a deep, cement-lined hole behind your house, just under the rain-water pipe. One morning you notice that a skunk has fallen in and is unable to get out.

You don't love skunks, but you wish them no harm. You also wish to get this one out of the cement-lined hole.

In a page or so, say how you did so.

THE CONFLICT between the men who make and the men who report the news is as old as time. News may be true, but it is not truth, and reporters and officials seldom see it the same way. The first great event, or Man in the News, was Adam, and the accounts of his creation have been the source of controversy ever since. In the old days, the reporters or couriers of bad news were often put to the gallows; now they are given the Pulitzer Prize, but the conflict goes on.

—JAMES RESTON, from *The Artillery of the Press*

1. At first sight, the statement from the above passage seems odd: "News may be true, but it is not truth."

But when you begin to think of it, it becomes less odd. Maybe it's true (if anything, as James Reston suggests, is true).

Write a paragraph or so giving the results of your thinking about the statement under discussion.

2. "The first great event, or Man in the News, was Adam," says Reston.

There must have been a first great event in your life. In a page or so, tell about it.

3. Your name is in the paper! The article tells how you were the heroic person whose selfless actions led to the saving of twenty lives.

You know this is not true. It only *seemed* true.

You argue with yourself. Should you inform the writer of the article that he was mistaken, that you were not in any way heroic, and that you performed no selfless actions? Should you urge him to write another article saying so?

In a page or so, recount that argument with yourself.

A REPORTER covering the police court learns that a certain policeman is going to be fired. He takes this information to the chief of police, who asks him to kill the story. The erring policeman has been found guilty of taking bribes from a gambler and has admitted his guilt. He is not going to be fired, but has resigned. The matter is settled, and airing it publicly will damage the public image of the police force and create suspicion of all police in the minds of the citizens. It may even be suggested that the police department expects cooperation from the reporter in return for the cooperation it gives him.

—DUANE BRADLEY, from *The Newspaper: Its Place in a Democracy*

1. A wallet full of money has been stolen from someone in your class. You know who did it. You go to that person, tell him that you know. He says, "Okay, I'll see that the wallet and the money are returned. Don't ask me how, and don't tell anyone that I did it."

The wallet and the money are returned. There is great mystery about it all.

In a page or so, say whether or not you'd tell who stole the wallet.

2. The last sentence in the above passage is an example of the old saying: "You scratch my back, I'll scratch yours."

In a few paragraphs, give an example of this sort of thing from your (or a friend's) experience.

3. In a page or so, tell of your being suspected of doing a certain thing which you hadn't done.

NEWSGATHERING

THE GREEN "START-THE-PRESS" light flashes. The great machines turn slowly. Pressmen move among the gigantic black frames, making sure each plate is impressing accurately on the web, or continuous ribbon of paper, flowing through the press. Then the "let go" signal is given. Faster and faster move the sheets of paper until the air is filled with thunderous roar.

Freshly printed papers climb in continuous streams up spring wire escalators to the mailroom, one floor above, at street level. Mailers whisk them from conveyor belts, run them through machines that automatically wrap, tie, and label them. Waiting delivery trucks speed them to trains, planes, and news dealers on the first leg of their journey to tomorrow's breakfast tables. —RUTH ADLER, from *The Working Press*

1. That's how it begins, your daily newspaper. In a page or so, recount the beginning of some daily routine in your life.

2. Surely you have known, or in some way come across, someone who was completely uninterested in the events of the world in which he lives, moves, and has his being—someone who is interested only in his own immediate problems, large or small.

In a page or so, give your conversation with that person when you tried your best to convey to him that the country of Neurotania had just dropped an atom bomb on the country of Impetigoland.

3. The editor of your school newspaper has just come to you and asked you to write a short article for the next issue, on any subject of interest to you.

In a few paragraphs, tell what you will write in that article.

NEWSGATHERING

A BELIEF AMONG ETHIOPIAN TRIBESMEN they will lose their souls if they are photographed was blamed today for an assault on Edward Genock, Paramount News cameraman, in Harar, Ethiopia.

Mr. Genock, who said he was unaware of the official ban on taking pictures in Harar, was set upon by warriors as he was making motion pictures of the arrival of Chief Arrisis and his followers. The natives smashed the camera and pummeled the operator before Chief Arrisis succeeded in calling them off. —from *The New York Times*, 1935

1. It is a very sad fact that many times we lose our tempers, or have our feelings hurt by the actions of someone. And yet, it turns out that the person had a very good, very logical reason for doing what he did. *And it had nothing at all to do with us.*

In a page or so, tell of such an incident in your experience (real or fictitious).

2. You are an Ethiopian tribesman. In a page or so, explain to a news cameraman why you fear you will lose your soul if he takes your picture.

3. What is your first thought upon realizing that it is Friday the thirteenth? You come to a ladder leaning against a house. Do you or do you not walk under or around it? You spill some salt. Do you or do you not throw a bit of it over your left shoulder?

In a few paragraphs, write upon one or all of the above questions.

NEWSGATHERING

Now, SUPPOSE YOU WERE BORN in a taxicab while your mother was on her way to the hospital. That makes more unusual news than being born in a hospital. A reporter, learning about your unusual place of birth, would probably have called your father or the doctor for more information. If the episode occurred in the middle of the night, while taxicabs were scarce, the story would have had still further interest. Other factors might have made the news of your birth more important if you were the first baby born in a new year, or if you were born on Christmas Day, or in a hurricane, or in the midst of some other catastrophe.

—DAVID BOTTER, from *News Reporters and What They Do*

1. The things we read in newspapers that make us really jump are the terrible things, the odd things, the smashups, the people getting into trouble. Whose heartbeats ever shot up after reading that the Jones family ate apple pie for supper and spent a quiet evening afterward?

In a paragraph or so for each, write two news stories concerning: (a) the most exciting (b) the dullest thing that happened in your area during the past week.

2. Suppose, as suggested at the beginning of the above passage, you had been born in a taxicab. In a page or so, say how that event influenced your life.

3. It is a fine, sunshiny, summer day. You are a reporter, traipsing around, looking for a story to write for your newspaper. You see (and hear!) a big argument going on between some parents and children on a lawn. A rake and a lawnmower lie on the ground. Neighbors have come to watch. Some have joined the battle. Fists have begun to fly.

In a page or so, write that story.

semantics

Hello wife, hello world, hello God,
I love you; hello certain monsters,
Ghosts, office buildings, I love you. Dog,
Dog-dogs, cat, cat-cats, I love you. . . .
Hello Things-in-Themselves, Things Not Quite
In Themselves (but trying), I love you . . .
            —ROBERT SWARD, from "Hello Poem"

1. What might the author of the above poem have meant when he wrote that he loves all those people and things? How can you love someone you've never even seen?

In a few paragraphs, say what you think he meant.

2. According to a critic, the above poem is an example of "beatnik poetry."

Beatnik, Hippie, or other names—who are these people who write happy poems, let their hair grow, wear flowers and maybe long robes, and all sorts of odd things?

In a page or so, give your answer to the above question.

3. During a page or so, be a person who is violently against the hippies, and say why they clutter up your world.

THERE WAS A TABLE set out under a tree in front of the house, and the March Hare and the Hatter were having tea at it: a Dormouse was sitting between them, fast asleep, and the other two were using it as a cushion, resting their elbows on it, and talking over its head. "Very uncomfortable for the Dormouse," thought Alice; "only as it's asleep, I suppose it doesn't mind."

The Hatter said, "Why is a raven like a writing-desk?"

"Come, we shall have some fun now!" thought Alice. "I'm glad they've begun asking riddles—I believe I can guess that," she added aloud.

"Do you mean that you think you can find out the answer to it?" said the March Hare.

"Exactly so," said Alice.

"Then you should say what you mean," the March Hare went on.

"I do," Alice hastily replied; "at least—at least I mean what I say —that's the same thing, you know."

"Not the same thing a bit!" said the Hatter. "Why, you might just as well say that 'I see what I eat' is the same thing as 'I eat what I see'!"

"You might just as well say," added the March Hare, "that 'I like what I get' is the same thing as 'I get what I like'!"

"You might just as well say," added the Dormouse, which seemed to be talking in its sleep, "that 'I breathe when I sleep' is the same thing as 'I sleep when I breathe'!"

"It *is* the same thing with you," said the Hatter, and here the conversation dropped, and the party sat silent for a minute, while Alice thought over all she could remember about ravens and writing-desks, which wasn't much.   —LEWIS CARROLL, from *Alice in Wonderland*

---

1. Perhaps you can think of an answer to the riddle which the Hatter asked Alice. Alice couldn't. A little later on in the book she asked the Hatter to tell her the answer, and he said: "I haven't the slightest idea."

Actually, it is easy to make up riddles which have no answers. But there are few people who have the courage to ask them. They are afraid that if they did, people might think them strange. People are accustomed to thinking that riddles should have answers, and that if a riddle didn't have an answer, no one should ask it.

However, the Hatter didn't seem to share this belief.

In a few paragraphs, describe someone you know (real or imaginary) who has the courage to do things that most people think strange.

2. Write a few riddles that have no answers.

■ SEMANTICS ■

"He flung himself from the room, flung himself upon his horse, and rode madly off in all directions."
—STEPHEN LEACOCK, from *Gertrude the Governess*

---

1. When you read that a person flings himself somewhere, you can't help but feel that he is exhibiting a certain lack of calm.

And when you read that he tosses himself upon his horse and rides off like a madman *in all directions at once*, even we the readers begin to puff a bit.

Try your skill. Write a page or so in which you convey an idea to your readers more by a word or phrase than by a direct description.

2. You are calm and sensible. You never lose your cool. You are confronted by an individual who is sputtering, trembling, feverish, and quite hectic.

Your purpose is to make this individual settle down.

In a page or so, report the dialogue which achieves this (or doesn't).

3. Speculate, during a few paragraphs, upon the following observation by a wit of the 1940's:

"People have more fun than anybody."

━━━━━━━━━━━━━━━ SEMANTICS ━━━━━━━━━━━━━━━

Epimenides the Cretan says, "All Cretans are liars." But Epimenides is himself a Cretan; therefore he is a liar himself. But if he is a liar, his statements are lies, and consequently the Cretans are veracious. But Epimenides is a Cretan, and, since they are veracious, what he says is true; and it follows after all that Cretans are liars.

—"Is Epimenides a Liar?"

---

veracious: truthful

---

1. Let us admit it: language can befuddle as well as unfuddle.

You have a friend who has read the above passage, has had difficulty in understanding it, and has come to you for an unfuddling.

In a few paragraphs, write the explanation that you will make to him.

2. You are a teacher. While you are taking the roll (and at a moment when your eye is fastened upon the strange costume of someone in the left rear of the room), a spitball flies with a hiss past your right ear.

Who threw it? You demand to know. Three voices, well distributed around the room, ring out: "I did!"

In a page or so, say how you will arrive at the truth of the matter.

3. Sometimes an occasion arises when a person has to make a difficult decision: should I or should I not tell the truth?

In a page or so, tell of such an occasion, and of your reasoned decision whether or not to tell the truth. The occasion may be real or fictional.

SEMANTICS

In the war for consumer favor ordinary standards of measurement quickly became inadequate. Giant Economy Size became the normal in package size and Large became the smallest unit on the shelves. Olives started with the "Giant" size and moved up quickly to "Mammoth," "Jumbo," "Colossal," and "Super Colossal." Low-line tires were "De Luxe" and moved up to "Super De Luxe," "Super Champion," and "Super Super." The pint was no longer a pint but a "large pint" and a gallon was no longer a gallon but a "big, big gallon." The quart and the pound similarly were found wanting and items were sold at such-and-such a price for "a full quart" or "a full pound."

In the same way the American Institute of Laundering advised member laundrymen to stay clear of such words as "grime, soiled, mildew, germs, dirt, and odor." To strike a happier note in their ads the laundry-men were supplied with a handbook which listed more than 300 friendlier words and phrases to use. Recommended were "abloom," "abundant," "youth," "zest," "help for the homemaker," "flower fresh," "silken loveli-ness," "longer wearing fabrics." And the ads could be brightened still more by a frequent sprinkling of colorful adjectives.

—JOSEPH J. SELDEN, from *The Golden Fleece*

---

1. What a strange world it is. Think of the hours you have listened to your teachers telling you exactly how the English language should be used. You've read textbooks, done homework, taken tests about it.

And yet, it seems, a person can use the English language quite differently from the way he was taught to use it, and get a good salary for doing so.

There are, surely, many things which we learn in school and have to relearn when we leave school. In a page or so, tell about one or more of these things.

2. In the school campaigns for elections of class officers it's tempting to make somewhat exaggerated claims for your candidate. If the claims are too exaggerated, people won't believe them. If they're too plain and simple, the other candidates will sound better.

Write a speech, presenting a candidate to the voters, telling how wonderful that candidate is, and what excellent work he is going to do for his constituents. But, at the same time, be careful not to "brag on him" too much. (Write a speech which will last about two minutes—about 300 words.)

How many of our fixed horrors—of blood, spiders, mice, snakes, thunderstorms, catching cold, darkness, enclosed places, tramps—are fears of words rather than of actual things, of an abstract "spider" rather than of real spiders weaving in a real world? How far can the semantic discipline dissolve these horrors, and restore to us a calm interpretation of our environment? I broke a mild case of snake horror by first studying the characteristics of snakes, then watching them at zoos, and finally allowing a friendly king snake—his name was Humphrey—to crawl up under my vest and out at my neck in the presence of a roomful of people to keep me steady. That ended that. I *experienced* snakes instead of worrying about Snakes with a capital S. —STUART CHASE, from *The Tyranny of Words*

---

1. You actively dislike someone, and decide to give that someone a bad time.

Using the ideas in the first few lines of the above passage, write out your plan for giving that someone a bad time.

2. You are a parent. One night you hear a series of screams from the bedroom of your four-year-old son. You rush in and find the child cowering in the corner of his bed, body distorted with sobs, face bleared with tears. What was wrong? Glim-Glom had made another visit!

You set your son upon your knee, you enfold him in your arms, you speak to him for ten minutes.

At the end of that ten minutes you put him back into bed. He goes to sleep immediately, smiling.

That was Glim-Glom's last visit.

What did you say to your four-year-old son during those ten minutes?

3. In one or more paragraphs, explain what Shakespeare meant when he wrote: ". . . 'tis the eye of childhood that fears a painted devil."

SEMANTICS

"That's the kind of coat which I'd like to know the person inside of it."

—ANONYMOUS

---

1. Are you an expert in English grammar? If so, explain what is wrong with the above sentence. If not, describe the coat, and the person inside of it.

2. Let's get down to the nitty-gritty. If you heard someone speaking in the manner of the quotation above, you'd very likely quake, either with laughter or with horror.

However, in order to thoroughly understand poor and ungrammatical speech, you really should be able to produce it. Do this. Write a speech of one page or so, which would make you quake (either with laughter or with horror) if you heard it delivered.

3. In great seriousness, write a few paragraphs giving your ideas as to the value of grammar to an individual's present and future life.

education

One impulse from a vernal wood
May teach you more of man,
Of moral evil and of good,
Than all the sages can.
—WILLIAM WORDSWORTH,
from "The Tables Turned"

---

vernal: occurring in the springtime. Thus, "vernal wood" is a wood in the springtime.

---

1. In a page or so, describe some of the "impulses" coming out of the woods in springtime. If you are a city person and have never seen the woods in springtime, tell about the springtime "impulses" you've noted in your environs.

2. Do you know the old line written by the poet Tennyson, "In the spring a young man's fancy lightly turns to thoughts of love"? Some witty person cut off the last part of this line, with the following result: "In the spring a young man's fancy."
In a page or so, discuss this.

3. In a few paragraphs, tell what you feel to have been the most important source of your education.

It was generally accepted that Professor Carver could identify any plant they brought in, whether he had seen it before or not, but his entomology class once rashly tried to hoodwink him. They produced a bug neatly pinned to a piece of cardboard and laid it on his desk.

"We just found this strange bug, Professor. What is it?"

He looked long at the curious creature. It had the head of a large ant, the body of a beetle, the legs of a spider, the antennae of a moth, all ingeniously put together. Finally he delivered his pronouncement, "Well, this, I think, is what we would call a humbug."

He liked pupils to do such things, and was delighted with the imagination that had fathered the hoax.

—RACKHAM HOLT, from *George Washington Carver*

---

1. He was a very skillful, learned man, Professor George Washington Carver. And he must also have had a fine friendly relationship with his students for them to try to fool him.

Of course, all students dearly dream of fooling their teachers. Have you ever made the attempt? Did the attempt fail, or was it successful?

Tell all about it (*all* about it!) in a page or so. If you never attempted to fool a teacher (and perhaps such a thing is possible), imagine that you did and write all about it.

2. Notice the last sentence of the passage: "He liked pupils to do such things [to try to fool him] and was delighted with the imagination that had fathered the hoax." This tells a great deal about George Washington Carver, as a teacher and as a man.

Imagine that you are a teacher whose class had done something of this sort. Tell about the "hoax," and about your reactions to it.

3. There are, in actuality, very strange bugs—very strange all sorts of things, for that matter. And surely you have seen some of them.

In a page or so, describe one of them (any one of them, from amoeba to man and everything in between) and tell something of your own reaction to it.

EDUCATION

ON THE MONDAY following his fourth birthday, our son spent his first day at school. When his mother and I greeted him at the end of the day, he said to her, "*Bonjour, madame,*" and then to me, "It's in French and it means hello.

"French," he said with authority, "is what they speak in another country. It's called France. It's far, far away. Some day I'll go there and I'll talk with them. In French. Because they don't understand our language. American." —HENRY GRIS, from foreword to *College Begins at Two*

---

1. Surely you've met them, these amazing young creatures who load you up with knowledge at the drop of a question.

In a few paragraphs, tell about an encounter with one.

2. Psychologists tell us that the "gifted child" is often an extremely lonely person, for his mind is just about adult, but his body is still immature. And so, except when he is with other gifted children, he is sort of "neither here nor there."

In a page or so, tell the thoughts of a gifted child upon being asked by the President of the PTA to give a talk before members of the Association.

3. Give your opinions concerning the following: "Every young man and woman should be given the opportunity to go to college."

EDUCATION

A MERELY WELL-INFORMED MAN is the most useless bore on God's earth. What we should aim at producing is men who possess both culture and expert knowledge in some special direction. Their expert knowledge will give them the ground to start from, and their culture will lead them as deep as philosophy and as high as art. We have to remember that the valuable intellectual development is self-development, and that it mostly takes place between the ages of sixteen and thirty. As to training, the most important part is given by mothers before the age of twelve.

—ALFRED NORTH WHITEHEAD, from "The Aims of Education"

1. No doubt at all. Someone who is "well-educated," who knows a lot of facts but not much else, and who never hesitates to let everyone know that he knows them, can grow a bit tiresome. In a page or so, tell about an enormous bore you've encountered.

2. In a page or so, tell about a fascinating person you've encountered at some point in your life.

3. You are the principal of a high school. Your school board has told you: "Go ahead and plan an entirely new curriculum for the school next year."

In a page or so, tell what old subjects you'd eliminate, what new subjects you'd introduce, and what new teaching methods you'd strive for.

Scene: the office in a corner of a large advertising agency somewhere East of Omaha. Seated at his desk munching tranquilizers is a frowning copywriter. He stares moodily at a small box lying before him. Wadded sheets of half-scribbled paper litter the floor.

Problem: he has to come up with an exciting new pitch for a dull old product. Well, the product isn't old, in name anyhow. It's another headache remedy. The ad man sighs and says to himself, "What can a guy do with acetylsalicylic acid that hasn't already been done?"

—RAY HUTCHINSON, from *The Gospel According to Madison Avenue*

---

1. Think of the plight of the man in the passage above. Suppose you were in a situation similar to his. You have already written four book reports on *The Adventures of Tom Sawyer* (or another book with which you are very familiar), and *all for the same teacher!* (This is, perhaps, a situation which could never be, but let's pretend it exists.)

So, this time your teacher says: "Okay, let's have it the fifth time, *but make it different this time!* If it's different I'll entertain the idea of giving you any mark up to 93. If it's the same I'll entertain the idea of giving you any mark up to 27."

Write this fifth book report on *The Adventures of Tom Sawyer* (or another book) pointing out exactly how and why this one is different from the other four. Do your best to earn a mark of 93.

2. Do you know anyone who falls for one advertisement after another? In several paragraphs tell about a few of their purchases and whether or not they tried to convince others to purchase the same articles.

3. Suppose you are the person about whom you told, just above. Describe one of the articles you bought, and tell why you liked it so much.

4. Perhaps you didn't like the article you bought. Tell the reasons why you didn't like it.

5. How do you picture the young man in the above passage (the copywriter chewing tranquilizers)? Write a two-hundred-word description of him. In the first hundred words describe him as he came into his office that morning. In the second hundred words describe him as he left his office that evening.

226

Then the whining schoolboy with his satchel
And shining morning face, creeping like snail
Unwillingly to school.
—WILLIAM SHAKESPEARE, from *As You Like It*

1. Shakespeare wrote the above lines nearly four hundred years ago. So, it would seem, some things haven't changed a great deal.

But why "unwillingly"? In a page or so, tell either of: (a) the most "unwilling" student you have ever known, or (b) the most willing.

2. In line two of the above passage is the phrase: "shining morning face." Apparently there has been some scrubbing here in getting ready for school.

In a page or so, tell of your experiences getting ready for school.

3. Suppose, by some terrible mishap, your feet didn't go the way you aimed them, and you found yourself not at school, but at some other place. In a few paragraphs, outline your decisions and actions immediately following this most distressing discovery.